YOUR could in our next cookbook!

Share your tried & true family favorites with us instantly at

www.gooseberrypatch.com

If you'd rather jot 'em down by hand, just mail this form to...
Gooseberry Patch • Cookbooks – Call for Recipes
PO Box 812 • Columbus, OH 43216-0812

If your recipe is selected for a book, you'll receive a FREE copy!

Please share only your original recipes or those that you have made your own over the years.

Recipe Name:

Number of Servings:

Any fond memories about this recipe? Special touches you like to add
or handy shortcuts?

Ingredients (include specific measurements):

Instructions (continue on back if needed):

Special Code: **cookbookspage**

Over ↗

Extra space for recipe if needed:

Tell us about yourself...

Your complete contact information is needed so that we can send you your FREE cookbook, if your recipe is published. Phone numbers and email addresses are kept private and will only be used if we have questions about your recipe.

Name:
Address:
City: State: Zip:
Email:
Daytime Phone:

Thank you! Vickie & JoAnn

Back-to-
SCHOOL
Fall Recipes

Delicious recipes to delight busy families, for every
autumn occasion from first day of school to Thanksgiving.

Gooseberry Patch

An imprint of Globe Pequot
246 Goose Lane
Guilford, CT 06437

www.gooseberrypatch.com
1•800•854•6673

Copyright 2020, Gooseberry Patch 978-1-62093-359-6

Do you have a tried & true recipe...

tip, craft or memory that you'd like to see featured in a **Gooseberry Patch** cookbook? Visit our website at **www.gooseberrypatch.com** and follow the easy steps to submit your favorite family recipe. Or send them to us at:

Gooseberry Patch
PO Box 812
Columbus, OH 43216-0812

Don't forget to include the number of servings your recipe makes, plus your name, address, phone number and email address. If we select your recipe, your name will appear right along with it... and you'll receive a **FREE** copy of the book!

Contents

Breakfasts for Busy Days...................... 5

Chilly-Day Soups & Breads...................33

Kid-Friendly Veggie Dishes................. 59

Family Favorites for Dinnertime......... 87

Pizzas, Burgers, Dogs & Tacos............121

Game-Day & After-School Snacks...... 155

Lunchbox Treats & Party Desserts.....183

Dedication

To all of our friends who believe that mealtime is family time, even on the busiest days of autumn.

Appreciation

Special thanks to all of you who shared your tried & true family favorites!

BREAKFASTS
for Busy Days

Back-to-School
FALL RECIPES

Ham & Egg Pizza

Charlotte Smith
Alexandria, PA

This is great breakfast food...everyone loves it, especially kids!
Very yummy and filling, yet easy to put together.

8-oz. tube refrigerated
   crescent rolls
2 c. cooked ham, finely chopped
1 c. frozen shredded hashbrowns
1 c. shredded Cheddar cheese

3 eggs, beaten
2 T. milk
1/8 t. pepper
1/2 c. shredded Parmesan
   cheese

Arrange crescent rolls on an ungreased 12" round pizza pan with points
to the center. Pinch together seams to form a crust; pinch the edge of
crust into a rim. Bake at 375 degrees for 5 minutes. Spread ham,
hashbrowns and Cheddar cheese over crust. In a bowl, whisk together
eggs, milk and pepper; carefully pour mixture over cheese. Sprinkle with
Parmesan cheese. Bake at 375 degrees for 25 to 30 minutes, until eggs
are completely set. Cut into wedges to serve. Makes 6 servings.

Good morning! Everyone knows that a good breakfast is
the best start to a day of school, work or play. So, let's
get a yummy breakfast on the table!

BREAKFASTS
for Busy Days

Beth's Egg & Chile Bake

Denise Webb
Newington, GA

Cheesy eggs with a southwestern flair! This simple egg dish is easy to mix together and bakes in 30 minutes. Beth is a friend from church, who has often brought this dish to our breakfasts before the Sunday service. Serve with extra salsa and warm corn muffins.

4-oz. can chopped green chiles, drained
1 c. favorite salsa, drained
1 doz. eggs, beaten
8-oz. pkg. shredded Cheddar cheese
8-oz. pkg. shredded Monterey Jack cheese
garlic salt to taste

Spread chiles and salsa in the bottom of a lightly greased 13"x9" baking pan. In a large bowl, whisk together eggs and cheeses; season generously with garlic salt. Spread egg mixture over salsa. Bake, uncovered, at 350 degrees for 30 minutes. Cut into squares to serve. Makes 8 servings.

Quick & Easy Home Fries

Shelley Turner
Boise, ID

Delicious made-from-scratch home fries aren't hard to make. So delicious with scrambled eggs and bacon.

3 to 4 russet potatoes, cubed
3 T. butter
1-1/2 T. olive oil
salt and pepper to taste

Rinse cubed potatoes with cold water; drain well and set aside. Melt butter with oil in a large skillet over medium heat. Add potatoes and stir to coat; season with salt and pepper. Cover and cook for 10 minutes. Uncover and stir; cook for another 10 minutes, turning often, until crisp and golden on all sides. Serves 4.

Cut up a plateful of scrambled eggs or pancakes in a jiffy using a pizza cutter.

Back-to-School
FALL RECIPES

Dark Chocolate Chip Pumpkin Muffins

Sara Voges
Washington, IN

*I love to share this recipe with family & friends...
everyone needs a good healthy breakfast treat!*

4 eggs, beaten
1 c. sugar
15-oz. can pumpkin
1 c. applesauce
1/2 c. oil
3 c. whole-wheat flour

2 t. baking powder
2 t. baking soda
1 t. salt
1 t. cinnamon
12-oz. pkg. dark chocolate chips

In a large bowl, combine eggs, sugar, pumpkin, applesauce and oil; beat until smooth. In another bowl, combine remaining ingredients except chocolate chips; mix well. Add flour mixture to egg mixture; stir well. Fold in chocolate chips. Spoon batter into 24 greased muffin cups, filling 3/4 full. Bake at 400 degrees for 16 to 20 minutes. Makes 2 dozen.

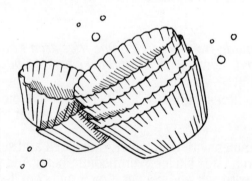

If you love freshly baked muffins, pick up a set of reusable silicone baking cups. They come in lots of bright kid-friendly colors and are also handy for other purposes like serving mini portions of fruit, nuts or chips.

BREAKFASTS
for Busy Days

Ham & Cheese Breakfast Bites

Paige Bear
Lyman, SC

This is a quick breakfast that's easily made ahead of time and reheated. I keep a bag of these in my fridge for my husband to eat.

4 eggs, beaten
1/2 c. milk or almond milk
1/4 c. biscuit baking mix
1/2 t. dried oregano
1/4 t. kosher salt
1/4 t. pepper

3/4 c. cooked ham, diced
2 green onions, chopped
1 tomato, chopped
3 T. shredded Cheddar cheese
1/2 c. favorite salsa, divided

In a large bowl, whisk together eggs, milk, baking mix and seasonings. Add ham, onions, tomato, cheese and 2 tablespoons salsa; mix well. Spoon egg mixture into 12 muffin cups sprayed with non-stick vegetable spray, filling almost full. Bake at 350 degrees for 35 minutes. Let stand in pan for another 5 minutes. Serve warm with remaining salsa. Makes one dozen.

There's a fall festival in our area that I attend every year with my daughters and granddaughter. There, they bake sticky buns and bread in a brick oven. We wait in line for hours for those yummy sticky buns! We get homemade apple butter, ham & bean soup and apple dumplings. After looking at all of the craft booths, we head to the next town to an old-fashioned train station for lunch and pick up some colorful potted mums at roadside markets on the way home. This is always the start of our fall season!

– Donna Burfield, Bellefonte, PA

Back-to-School
FALL RECIPES

Apple & Banana Griddle Cakes

Jackie Smulski
Lyons, IL

Your family will love these hearty, fruit-filled pancakes.

1 Gala apple, peeled, cored
   and diced
1 Granny Smith apple, peeled,
   cored and diced
1 T. butter
1/2 c. all-purpose flour
1/2 c. whole-wheat flour
1/2 t. baking soda

1/2 c. milk
2 egg whites, beaten
1 egg yolk, beaten
2 to 3 T. water
1 to 2 ripe bananas, thinly sliced
Garnish: additional butter,
   pancake syrup

In a skillet over medium heat, sauté apples in butter until tender. Meanwhile, in a large bowl, combine flours, baking soda, milk, egg whites and egg yolk. Mix well; stir in enough water to make a pancake batter consistency. Fold in sliced bananas and sautéed apples. Spoon batter by 1/2 cupfuls onto a greased hot griddle or skillet until bubbles pop up on top of pancakes. Flip and cook on other side until done. Serve griddle cakes warm with butter and syrup. Makes 10 to 12 pancakes.

Waffles and pancakes can be frozen in plastic freezer bags
for up to a month. Reheat them in a toaster or microwave for
a quick homestyle breakfast on busy weekdays.

BREAKFASTS
for Busy Days

Peanut Butter & Jelly Pancakes

Robin Hill
Rochester, NY

My kids hurry to breakfast when these pancakes are on the griddle!
Grape jelly is an old favorite, but they've enjoyed trying strawberry,
blueberry and even raspberry jam with these too.

2 c. pancake mix
1-1/2 c. water
1 egg, beaten
2 T. oil

1/2 c. creamy peanut butter
Garnish: favorite jelly or jam
Optional: additional peanut
    butter

In a large bowl, combine pancake mix, water, egg and oil; stir until smooth and set aside. Spoon peanut butter into a microwave-safe cup. Microwave for 30 seconds to one minute; stir until smooth and mix into batter. Ladle batter by 1/4 to 1/2 cupfuls onto a hot greased griddle or skillet. Cook until bubbles form on top; turn over and cook until golden on the bottom. Serve pancakes topped with jelly or jam and additional peanut butter, if desired. Serves 4.

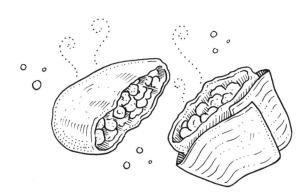

Is the school bus on the way? Fill a pita pocket with a favorite breakfast food...scrambled eggs, a sausage patty and cheese or even sliced bananas with peanut butter. Wrap it up in a paper towel and they're set to go!

Back-to-School
FALL RECIPES

Fruity Breakfast Sundae

Lisa Ann Panzino DiNunzio
Vineland, NJ

This fruity sundae is healthy, refreshing and a snap to make!
This recipe serves one, but it's so easy to double.

6-oz. container plain or vanilla
   Greek yogurt
honey or maple syrup to taste
1/4 c. fresh blueberries

1/4 c. fresh strawberries, hulled
   and sliced
1/4 c. granola cereal

Spoon yogurt into a small bowl; stir in honey or syrup to taste. In a clear glass tumbler or small canning jar, layer half each of yogurt, blueberries, strawberries and granola. Repeat layers, ending with granola. Serve immediately. Makes one serving.

Cinnamon-Oat Granola

Marian Forck
Chamois, MO

I love to sprinkle granola on my yogurt. We serve this at the school where I work, where it's made twice a week. I make it at home too. It's good sprinkled over fresh fruit or ice cream too.

3 c. rolled oats, uncooked
1 c. brown sugar, packed

2 T. cinnamon
1/2 to 3/4 c. butter, melted

Combine oats, brown sugar and cinnamon in a bowl; toss to mix well. Gradually stir in 1/2 cup melted butter, adding more butter if needed to moisten well. Spread into a lightly greased 15"x10" jelly-roll baking pan. Bake at 350 degrees for 18 minutes, or until crisp. Cool; store in an airtight container. Makes 30 servings.

Some old-fashioned things like fresh air
and sunshine are hard to beat.

– Laura Ingalls Wilder

BREAKFASTS
for Busy Days

Blast of Sunshine Smoothies

Joyceann Dreibelbis
Wooster, OH

This smoothie is so bright, cheerful and delicious, it will brighten even the most rainy, windy days! A great breakfast on the run. You can swap out the mango with strawberries for a change.

1 mango, peeled, pitted
   and cubed
1 banana, sliced
1 c. orange juice

1 c. vanilla yogurt
cinnamon to taste
Optional: 1 to 2 c. ice cubes

Add all ingredients to a blender; process until smooth. Pour into glasses and serve. Makes 4 servings.

Berries & Cream Smoothies

Sonya Labbe
Quebec, Canada

This delicious smoothie is made with yogurt and frozen berries. Since it uses frozen fruit, you can enjoy it year 'round, even in wintertime.

1 c. vanilla yogurt
1/4 c. milk
3/4 c. frozen strawberries

1/2 c. frozen raspberries
1/4 c. frozen blueberries
2 c. ice cubes

Combine all ingredients in a blender; process until smooth. Pour into glasses and serve. Makes 2 to 3 servings.

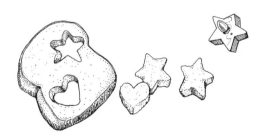

Serving up toast to finicky kids? Cut toast into whimsical shapes with cookie cutters. Spread with nut butter or fruit jam...sure to be a hit!

Back-to-School FALL RECIPES

Meat Lovers' Quiche

Beth Flack
Terre Haute, IN

This hearty breakfast pie is great for tailgating brunches...
good for dinner with a tossed salad too.

8-inch deep-dish pie crust,
thawed if frozen
6 slices bacon, crisply cooked
and crumbled
1 c. ground pork breakfast
sausage, browned and
drained

1/2 c. cooked ham, diced
1/2 c. onion, diced
1 c. shredded Swiss cheese
6 eggs, well beaten
1/2 c. milk
1/4 t. salt
1/8 t. pepper

Set pie crust on a baking sheet; pierce crust all over with a fork. Bake at 425 degrees for 10 minutes; let cool for a few minutes. Sprinkle bacon, sausage, ham, onion and cheese evenly into crust. In a large bowl, whisk together remaining ingredients; pour into crust. Bake for 425 degrees for 20 minutes, or until center is set and a toothpick inserted in the center comes out clean. Let stand for 10 minutes before slicing. Serves 8.

Crescent Breakfast Squares

Candy Winters
Jacksonville, IL

My family loves sausage and cheese, so this is perfect for us. Their motto is always, "You can never have too much cheese!"

1 lb. mild ground pork sausage
8-oz. pkg cream cheese, softened
2 8-oz. tubes refrigerated
crescent rolls

2 to 3 c. shredded Cheddar
cheese

Brown sausage in a skillet over medium heat; drain. Add cream cheese to sausage in skillet. Cook over low heat, stirring often, until cream cheese melts. Meanwhile, unroll one tube of rolls; press into the bottom and 1/2-inch up the sides of a lightly greased 13"x9" glass baking pan. Spoon sausage mixture into pan; sprinkle with Cheddar cheese. Unroll second tube of rolls; arrange on top. Bake, uncovered, at 375 degrees for about 20 minutes, until golden. Cool for 15 minutes; cut into squares. Serves 8 to 10.

BREAKFASTS
for Busy Days

Madge's Favorite Breakfast Bake

Sandy Coffey
Cincinnati, OH

This dish has been a family favorite for years for our holiday breakfasts and brunches. It's a recipe that everyone loves, from young to old. Serve with warm biscuits and honey and you have a scrumptious breakfast for any occasion. To serve a smaller group, halve the recipe and use a 9"x9" pan.

1 lb. ground pork breakfast
   sausage
4 lbs. redskin potatoes, cubed
1 yellow onion, diced

10 eggs, lightly beaten
8-oz. pkg. shredded Cheddar
   cheese, divided
salt and pepper to taste

Pull apart uncooked sausage into teaspoon-size pieces; place in a large bowl. Add potatoes, onion, eggs and one cup cheese; stir gently. Season with salt and pepper. Spread mixture in a lightly greased 13"x9" deep baking pan. Sprinkle remaining cheese on top. Cover tightly with aluminum foil. Bake at 325 degrees for about one hour, until eggs are set and potatoes are fork-tender. Makes 8 to 10 servings.

Tickle the kids with Jack-o'-Lantern oranges for breakfast. Slice the tops off navel oranges and scoop out the pulp with a spoon. Draw on silly or spooky faces with food coloring markers. Spoon in fruit salad and serve...clever!

Oven-Baked Cinnamon French Toast

Gladys Kielar
Whitehouse, OH

This French toast tastes really special, but it's simple to make. Any leftovers can be wrapped and frozen. To serve, let frozen toast come to room temperature, arrange on a baking sheet and bake at 350 degrees until heated through.

12 slices cinnamon-raisin bread
2 eggs, beaten
16-oz. container half-and-half or
   light cream
6 T. margarine, melted and
   cooled slightly

2 T. brown sugar, packed
2 t. vanilla extract
1/4 t. cinnamon
Optional: 1 t. orange zest,
   1/8 t. nutmeg
Garnish: powdered sugar

In a lightly greased 13"x9" baking pan, arrange bread slices in 2 layers; set aside. In a large bowl, combine remaining ingredients except garnish; whisk until well blended. Pour egg mixture evenly over bread slices; press bread down until some of the liquid is absorbed. Bake, uncovered, at 350 degrees for 45 minutes, or until golden. Cut into squares; sprinkle with powdered sugar. Serves 6.

Breakfast sliders! Whip up your favorite pancake batter and make silver dollar-size pancakes. Sandwich them together with slices of heat & serve sausage. Serve with maple syrup on the side for dipping...yum!

BREAKFASTS
for Busy Days

Overnight French Toast with Berry Sauce

Sonya Labbe
Quebec, Canada

This is delicious for breakfast and brunch. Since it's refrigerated overnight, it's a great make-ahead...in the morning, bake and serve.

4 eggs
1-1/2 c. whole milk
1/2 c. sugar, divided
1 t. vanilla extract
1/8 t. salt

4 thick slices brioche or other
   egg bread
2 T. butter, melted
10-oz. pkg. frozen mixed berries,
   thawed

In a 13"x9" baking pan, whisk together eggs, milk, 1/4 cup sugar, vanilla and salt. Arrange bread in pan in a single layer; let soak for 15 minutes. Turn bread over; cover and refrigerate overnight. Brush a rimmed baking sheet with melted butter. With a spatula, carefully transfer soaked bread to sheet. Bake, uncovered, at 350 degrees for 25 to 30 minutes, until set in the center and lightly golden on the bottom. Meanwhile, in a bowl, combine berries and remaining sugar, mashing lightly with a fork. To serve, remove French toast from baking sheet with a spatula; top with berry mixture. Makes 4 servings.

Are the refrigerator doors overwhelmed with crayon masterpieces? Select a few special drawings to have matted and framed...the kids will be so proud!

Back-to-School
FALL RECIPES

Pumpkin Pie Baked Oatmeal

Marsha Baker
Pioneer, OH

I love all kinds of baked oatmeal! We don't wait until autumn to enjoy this healthy start to the day. It's moist and oh-so delicious. It reheats well, for a quick breakfast another day.

1 c. canned pumpkin
2 eggs, beaten
1 c. apple cider or juice
1/2 c. milk
1/4 c. honey
2 T. pure maple syrup
2 T. butter, melted
1 t. vanilla extract

2 t. pumpkin pie spice
1-3/4 c. rolled oats, uncooked
1-1/2 t. baking powder
1/8 t. baking soda
1/4 t. salt
1/2 c. pecan halves
Optional: maple syrup or honey,
   warmed

In a large bowl, combine pumpkin, eggs, cider, milk, honey, syrup, butter, vanilla and spice; whisk together until smooth. Stir in oats, baking powder, baking soda and salt. Spray an 8"x8" baking pan with non-stick vegetable spray. Spoon oat mixture into pan; sprinkle with pecans. Bake at 350 degrees for 40 to 45 minutes, until heated through. Serve with warm maple syrup or honey, if desired. Makes 8 servings.

Fill a muffin tin with yummy oatmeal toppings...brown sugar, raisins, chopped nuts and even chocolate chips. So easy for everyone to help themselves! The muffin tin can be wrapped in plastic for serving again another day.

BREAKFASTS
for Busy Days

Cranberry-Pecan Instant Oatmeal Mix

Sherry Sheehan
Evensville, TN

I created this when I was working an early-morning shift and wanted something easy yet healthy for first break. For variety, you can substitute different combinations of dried fruits and nuts.

8 c. rolled oats, uncooked
1 c. dried cranberries
1 c. brown sugar, packed
1 c. powdered milk

1/2 c. chopped pecans
1 T. cinnamon
1 t. salt
Optional: milk

Combine all ingredients except optional milk in a bowl; mix well. Divide among 8 plastic zipping sandwich bags; close bags and store in an airtight container. To make one serving: Pour one packet of oatmeal mix into a microwave-safe bowl; add 1/2 cup water. Microwave on high for 2 minutes. Let stand 3 to 4 minutes. If desired, top with milk. Makes 8 servings.

Exciting Oatmeal Breakfast

Randy Larson
Indian Harbour Beach, FL

I like this meal because it's quick, warm and fun. For a spicy variation, instead of the spices, add 1/2 cup creamy peanut butter.

5 c. milk or water
1/4 t. salt
1 t. cinnamon
1/2 tsp. ground ginger

1/2 t. allspice
1/4 t. nutmeg
3 c. quick-cooking oats,
   uncooked

In a large saucepan over medium heat, bring milk or water and salt to a rolling boil. Add spices and oats; stir well. Cook for one minute, stirring occasionally. Cover and remove from heat; let stand 2 to 3 minutes and serve. Serves 6.

Back-to-School
FALL RECIPES

Beckie's Brunch Bake

Beckie Apple
Grannis, AR

My husband and I love to share this easy, all-in-one dish on the weekend and then microwave the leftovers for early weekday breakfasts. It's also a favorite for big family get-togethers.

3 T. butter
1/4 c. green pepper, diced
1/4 c. onion, diced
8 eggs, beaten
2 c. milk
1/8 t. garlic powder
1/8 t. Italian seasoning
1/8 t. salt

1/8 t. pepper
8-oz. pkg. shredded Cheddar
  cheese
6-oz. can chunk ham, drained
  and finely diced
1 tomato, coarsely chopped
4-oz. can sliced mushrooms

In a microwave-safe 2-quart bowl, combine butter, green pepper and onion; microwave on high for 4 minutes. Add eggs, milk and seasonings; whisk until well mixed. Gently stir in cheese, ham, tomato and mushrooms with liquid; mix well. Spread mixture evenly in a 13"x9" baking pan sprayed with non-stick vegetable spray. Bake, uncovered, at 375 degrees for 25 to 30 minutes, until lightly golden and a toothpick inserted in the center comes out clean. Let stand for 10 minutes; cut into squares. Serves 8 to 10.

Serve up Egg in a Nest for a special breakfast. Cut out the center of a slice of bread. Add the bread to a buttered skillet over medium heat and break an egg into the hole. Cook until golden on the bottom; turn over with a spatula and cook until the egg is set.

BREAKFASTS
for Busy Days

Mom's Banana Tea Bread

Kathy Courington
Canton, GA

Growing up, I loved the smell of this bread in the oven. My mother loved to bake and this is one of her best recipes. So yummy enjoyed warm with butter and a cup of hot tea or cocoa.

1-3/4 c. all purpose flour	1/3 c. shortening
2 t. baking powder	2/3 c. sugar
1/4 t. baking soda	2 eggs, lightly beaten
1/2 t. salt	1 c. ripe banana, mashed

In a bowl, sift together flour, baking powder, baking soda and salt; set aside. In a separate bowl, blend together shortening and sugar; add eggs and beat well. Blend flour mixture into shortening mixture; fold in banana. Pour batter into a greased and floured 9"x5" loaf pan. Bake at 350 degrees for 50 minutes, or until a toothpick inserted in the center comes out clean. Turn loaf out of pan; cool on a wire rack. Makes one loaf.

My mom was a frugal farmer's wife. We didn't have much, but we didn't know that, because Mom always "made do." One of the fond memories of my childhood is picking bushels of apples ourselves from a local orchard, then taking them to the basement, where Dad had hauled in a horse watering tank. We wrapped each apple individually in newspapers, to keep the rest from spoiling when one apple decided to spoil. It seemed like an all-day job, but oh, how we always cherished Mom's apple pies and apple dumplings! On a busy baking day, my brothers and I had no idea how blessed we were to get to enjoy apple dumplings for dinner...not dessert!

– Marsha Baker, Pioneer, OH

Back-to-School
FALL RECIPES

Quick Avocado-Egg Breakfast Sandwich

Constance Bockstoce
Dallas, GA

In a hurry? This recipe takes just minutes and is easy to take along.

1 English muffin, split
1 egg
1/4 avocado, peeled, pitted
   and sliced

salt and pepper to taste

Toast English muffin. Meanwhile, lightly oil a 3" to 4" glass ramekin. Break egg into ramekin; break yolk with a fork. Cover with a paper towel; microwave on high for 30 to 45 seconds, until egg is completely cooked. Mash avocado onto one muffin half with a fork; carefully top avocado with cooked egg. Season with salt and pepper; top with remaining muffin half. Wrap sandwich in a napkin and serve. Makes one sandwich.

Sausage Breakfast Muffins

Tracy Stoll
Seville, OH

We make these on special mornings. Quick & easy, and they taste so good...great with crispy bacon too!

10-oz. tube refrigerated biscuits,
   separated
1/4 lb. ground pork breakfast
   sausage, browned and
   drained

1/2 c. shredded Cheddar cheese
5 eggs
1/2 c. milk

Flatten biscuits with a rolling pin; press into greased muffin cups. Divide sausage and cheese among cups. Beat eggs with milk; pour evenly into cups. Bake at 350 degrees for 20 to 25 minutes, until eggs are set. Serve warm. Makes 10 muffins.

Set the breakfast table the night before...enjoy a
relaxed breakfast in the morning.

22

BREAKFASTS
for Busy Days

Mini Breakfast Quiches

Liz Blackstone
Racine, WI

My son thought "quiche" sounded too fancy, but when I called them "breakfast pies" he gobbled them up! Feel free to mix & match the veggies and cheese in the filling...it's always delicious. Great for tailgating buffets too!

12-oz. tube refrigerated
    buttermilk biscuits, separated
2/3 c. shredded Swiss cheese
1/3 c. cooked ham, finely
    chopped
1/4 c. green onion, finely
    chopped

3 eggs, beaten
2 T. milk
1/4 t. salt
1/8 t. pepper

Flatten biscuits on a lightly floured surface. Place each biscuit in a greased muffin cup. Press into bottoms and sides of cups and form a rim at top; set aside. Combine cheese, ham and onions in a small bowl; mix well and spoon 2 tablespoons of mixture into each cup. In another bowl, whisk together eggs, milk, salt and pepper. Spoon egg mixture into cups, dividing evenly. Bake at 350 degrees for 20 to 25 minutes, until eggs are set and biscuits are deeply golden. Serve warm. Makes 10 servings.

Deliver a tray of your favorite breakfast goodies to the
teachers' lounge at school...it's sure to be appreciated!

Back-to-School
FALL RECIPES

Golden Waffles

Vickie
Gooseberry Patch

Nothing inspires morning smiles like the unmistakable scent of waffles for breakfast!

2 c. all-purpose flour
1 T. baking powder
1 T. sugar
1/2 t. salt
3 eggs, separated

1-1/2 c. milk
5 T. shortening, melted
Garnish: butter, pancake syrup or
   powdered sugar

In a large bowl, stir together flour, baking powder, sugar and salt; set aside. In a separate bowl, beat together egg yolks, milk and shortening; blend into flour mixture until smooth. In another bowl, beat egg whites with an electric mixer on high setting until stiff peaks form; fold into batter. Pour 1/2 cup batter per waffle onto a greased, preheated waffle iron; bake as manufacturer directs. Garnish as desired. Serves 6.

Amish Fried Apples

Marcia Shaffer
Conneaut Lake, PA

These apples go very well with breakfast sausages, baked ham and roast pork. I've found that Jonathan apples are the best for this recipe, as they keep their shape while becoming tender.

1/4 c. butter
6 c. Jonathan apples, cored
   and sliced
2 T. sugar

2 T. brown sugar, packed
1/2 t. lemon zest
1/4 t. salt

Melt butter in a skillet over medium heat. Add apples; sprinkle with remaining ingredients and stir. Cook for 10 minutes, turning apples carefully with a spatula, until tender. Serve warm. Makes 4 to 6 servings.

Stir a sprinkle of wheat germ into pancake batter or oatmeal for a nutty taste that's healthy too.

BREAKFASTS
for Busy Days

Scrambled Eggs with Mushrooms & Swiss

Grace Smith
British Columbia, Canada

Scrambled eggs are just about the easiest breakfast dish ever!

4 eggs	1/2 c. mushrooms, chopped
salt and pepper to taste	1/2 c. baby spinach, chopped
2 t. butter	2 to 3 T. shredded Swiss cheese

In a small bowl, whisk together eggs, salt and pepper until blended; set aside. In a skillet, melt butter over medium-high heat. Add mushrooms; cook and stir for 3 to 4 minutes, until tender. Add spinach; cook and stir until wilted. Reduce heat to medium; pour in egg mixture. Cook and stir just until eggs are set. Sprinkle with cheese; let stand until melted. Makes 2 servings.

Mini Egg & Cheese Bites

Jen Thomas
Santa Rosa, CA

These cute little golden disks of egg and cheese are perfect for children. Easy to freeze for another day!

6 eggs	salt and pepper to taste
3 T. milk	1/3 c. shredded Cheddar cheese

In a bowl, whisk together eggs, milk, salt and pepper. Pour into greased mini muffin cups, filling 2/3 full; top with cheese. Bake at 350 degrees for 8 to 10 minutes, until set. Let cool in pan for a few minutes; remove to a wire rack. Serve immediately, or cool completely, wrap in plastic wrap and freeze. To serve, microwave for 15 to 30 seconds, until heated through. Makes about one dozen.

Back-to-School
FALL RECIPES

Mama P's Sour Cream Pancakes
Daisy Sedalnick
Westminster, CO

These are amazing! Once you've tasted these pancakes, you will never want any other kind. This recipe came to me from my sister, who got it from her mother-in-law. Pour on your favorite pancake topping and enjoy.

3/4 c. all-purpose flour
2 t. baking powder
1/2 t. salt

4 eggs, well beaten
16-oz. container sour cream

In a large bowl, mix flour, baking powder and salt. In a separate bowl, blend eggs and sour cream. Stir egg mixture into flour mixture, being careful not to overmix. Pour 2 tablespoons batter per pancake onto a hot greased griddle. Cook until bubbles forming on top start to pop. Turn over; cook just a little longer. Serves 3 to 4.

Cinnamon Pull-Aparts
Patty Flak
Erie, PA

These warm cinnamon rolls smell amazing when they're baking! We love them for Christmas, but they're simple enough to make any breakfast special. Kids love to pull them apart.

1/3 c. plus 1/2 c. sugar, divided
3/4 t. cinnamon, divided
2 7-1/2 oz. tubes refrigerated
   biscuits, quartered

1/3 c. butter, melted

In a bowl, combine 1/3 cup sugar and 1/4 teaspoon cinnamon. Roll biscuit quarters in sugar mixture; place in a greased 9"x5" loaf pan. Combine melted butter and remaining sugar and cinnamon; drizzle over biscuits in pan. Bake at 350 degrees for 35 to 40 minutes. To serve, flip pan upside-down onto a serving plate. Makes 8 servings.

On weekends, enjoy breakfast outdoors! Spread out a quilt and enjoy the cool morning air.

Apple-Filled Coffee Cake

Stephanie Nilsen
Fremont, NE

This recipe has been a huge hit at church breakfasts, and I'm asked for the recipe whenever I bring it. It's moist and filled with flavor! Cherry pie filling is good in this too. This cake really needs no icing. However, if you like, you can drizzle it with one cup powdered sugar mixed with one to 2 tablespoons milk.

1/2 c. brown sugar, packed	4 eggs, beaten
1/4 c. cinnamon	1/2 c. oil
18-1/2 oz. pkg. yellow cake mix	1/4 c. water
3-oz. pkg. instant vanilla	8-oz. container sour cream
pudding mix	21-oz. can apple pie filling

Combine brown sugar and cinnamon in a cup; set aside. In a large bowl, combine dry cake and pudding mixes, eggs, oil, water and sour cream. Mix well; batter will be a little thick. Grease a Bundt® pan with shortening; sprinkle with flour. Spoon half of batter evenly into pan; sprinkle with half of brown sugar mixture. Slice through batter with a table knife to swirl in brown sugar mixture. Spoon pie filling over top. Spoon remaining batter over pie filling; add remaining brown sugar mixture and swirl with knife. Bake at 350 degrees for 50 minutes, or until a toothpick inserted near the center tests clean. Set cake in pan on a wire rack; cool. Invert onto a serving plate; slice and serve. Serves 12 to 16.

Make banana pops for breakfast! Insert treat sticks in bananas. Spread with fruit-flavored yogurt, roll in cereal and place on a tray to freeze. Wrap in plastic wrap and return to freezer for a cool treat kids are sure to love.

Back-to-School
FALL RECIPES

Marshmallow Puffs

Claire Martin
Salina, KS

Light and airy, these puffs are a breakfast treat with milk.
They're delicious with afternoon coffee too.

1/4 c. brown sugar, packed
1/2 t. cinnamon
8 marshmallows
1/4 c. butter, melted
8-oz. tube refrigerated
   crescent rolls

1/4 c. powdered sugar
1/4 t. vanilla extract
2 t. milk

Combine brown sugar and cinnamon in a cup. For each puff, dip a marshmallow in melted butter; roll in cinnamon-sugar. Lay marshmallow on a crescent roll and wrap it up, completely covering marshmallow. Squeeze edges of dough to seal. Dip roll in melted butter; place in a greased muffin cup. Fill empty muffin cups 1/3 full of water for even baking. Bake at 375 degrees for 10 to 15 minutes, until golden. In a small bowl, mix remaining ingredients; drizzle over puffs. Serve warm. Makes 4 servings, 2 puffs each.

Make breakfast fun for kids! Let them create smiley faces on bagels using cream cheese and sliced fruit...serve milk or juice with twisty straws.

BREAKFASTS
for Busy Days

No-Bake Energy Bites

Julie Wiesen
Houston, TX

We found these at a small coffee shop on a trip to the mountains of North Carolina. They're addicting! Perfect when you need something healthy on the go.

1 c. rolled oats, uncooked	1/3 c. honey
2/3 c. flaked coconut, toasted	3 T. ground flax seed
1/2 c. creamy peanut butter	1 t. vanilla extract
1/2 c. semi-sweet chocolate chips	

Stir all ingredients together in a bowl until thoroughly mixed. Cover and chill in refrigerator for 30 minutes. Roll into one-inch balls; store in an airtight container. May keep refrigerated up to one week. Makes 1-1/2 to 2 dozen.

I have been sewing all of my life, it seems. When my daughter Jenny started school, I stitched a new dress for her first day. It was brown and blue plaid cotton. She called it her "tea dress" as it reminded her of my many cups of tea that I would drink while sewing. She still remembers her tea dress from grade one. She is now in her 40s, with her own little girl who may someday have a new "tea dress" of her own.

— Dawn Saunders, New Brunswick, Canada

Back-to-School
FALL RECIPES

Chocolate-Banana Overnight Oats

Marla Kinnersley
Surprise, AZ

We love waking up to this super-delicious, healthy breakfast.
We put it together the night before, then in the morning we just
stir in the sliced bananas and peanut butter...and enjoy!

1 c. old-fashioned oats,
  uncooked and divided
1 c. unsweetened vanilla almond
  milk, divided
4 T. baking cocoa

4 T. honey
4 t. chia seed
1-1/3 t. vanilla extract
1 ripe banana, thinly sliced
4 T. creamy peanut butter

To each of 4 mini canning jars or cereal bowls, add 1/4 cup oats and
1/4 cup milk; stir. Divide cocoa, honey, chia seed and vanilla among
jars; stir well. Cover and refrigerate overnight. In the morning, divide
banana slices among jars; top evenly with peanut butter and serve.
Makes 4 servings.

Hard-boiled eggs are terrific to have on hand for speedy
breakfasts, easy sandwiches or even a quick nutritious snack.
Use eggs that have been refrigerated at least 7 to 10 days...
the shells will slip right off.

BREAKFASTS
for Busy Days

Skillet Breakfast Casserole

Sarah Slaven
Strunk, KY

This hearty dish is one of my family's favorite meals. We not only eat it for breakfast, we love it for dinner just as much.

4 c. frozen diced hashbrowns
3 T. oil
1 lb. ground pork breakfast
   sausage
2.6-oz. pkg. country sausage
   gravy mix

2 eggs, beaten
8-oz. pkg. shredded Colby Jack
   cheese

In a skillet, cook hashbrowns with oil as package directs; transfer to a 2-quart casserole dish. In same skillet over medium heat, brown sausage and drain, reserving drippings in skillet. Spoon sausage over hashbrowns; set aside. In reserved drippings in skillet, prepare gravy mix according to package directions. Stir beaten eggs into gravy. Pour gravy mixture over sausage in casserole dish; top with cheese. Cover and bake at 350 degrees for 45 minutes. Uncover and bake another 15 minutes, until bubbly and cheese is golden. Makes 6 servings.

Start a tailgating Saturday right...invite friends to join you for breakfast. Let the kids ask a friend, too. Keep it simple with a breakfast casserole, baskets of muffins and a fresh fruit salad. It's all about food and friends!

Back-to-School
FALL RECIPES

Omelet in a Bag

Joan Chance
Houston, TX

My grandchildren like to make this omelet, fixing it just the way they like. It works so well on camping trips together...fun to do at home too! Up to 6 bags can go into the pot at once.

2 eggs
1 T. water
1 T. favorite shredded cheese
1 T. cooked ham or bacon, diced

Optional: chopped onion,
   mushrooms, tomato
Garnish: salsa, sour cream

Bring a large pot of water to a boil. Meanwhile, crack eggs into a one-quart heavy-duty plastic freezer bag; add water. Seal bag and shake or squeeze the bag to mix eggs well. Add other ingredients as desired. Press as much air out of the bag as possible; seal tightly. Press bag to evenly distribute egg mixture. Carefully add bag to the boiling water; simmer for 11 to 13 minutes, until set. Slide omelet out onto a plate; add desired toppings. Serves one.

Speedy Breakfast Burrito

Tonya Sheppard
Galveston, TX

I call these my "out the door, the bus is coming" burritos!

2 eggs
salt and pepper to taste
2 10-inch flour tortillas

2 slices American or Cheddar
   cheese
2 t. salsa

Beat eggs with salt and pepper in a microwave-safe bowl sprayed with non-stick vegetable spray. Microwave on high for about 90 seconds, stirring every 30 seconds, until set. Slice cooked eggs in half. Top each tortilla with one piece of egg, a cheese slice and one teaspoon salsa. Fold in sides of tortillas; roll up burrito-style. Microwave on high for 20 seconds, or until cheese melts. Wrap in a paper towel and serve. Serves 2.

Chilly-Day
SOUPS &
BREADS

Back-to-School
FALL RECIPES

Good-For-You Chili

Linda Payne
Snow Hill, MD

This recipe is great! You can enjoy a delicious bowl of chili, or use it to top a baked potato or sweet potato fries. To make it extra good, top with a little shredded cheese.

1 lb. lean ground beef
2 to 3 t. oil
3/4 c. onion, chopped
1 T. garlic, minced
2 14-1/2 oz. cans fire-roasted
   diced tomatoes

2 16-oz. cans black beans
1 T. chili powder
1 t. ground cumin
salt and pepper to taste
Optional: reduced-fat or regular
   shredded cheese

Brown beef in a large skillet over medium heat; drain and set aside. To the same skillet, add oil, onion and garlic; cook over low heat for 3 to 5 minutes. Add tomatoes with juice, beans and seasonings; return beef mixture to skillet. Bring to a boil over medium heat; simmer for 10 to 15 minutes. At serving time, top with cheese, if desired. Makes 8 servings.

Start a delicious soup supper tradition on Halloween night. Soup stays simmering hot while you hand out treats, and it isn't too filling, so everyone has more room to nibble on goodies!

Chilly-Day
SOUPS & BREADS

Chicken & Vegetable
Tortellini Soup

Anne Alesauskas
Minocqua, WI

This is a wonderful soup...add any fresh veggies that are in season.

2 T. olive oil
1/2 c. onion, diced
1/2 c. carrot, peeled and diced
3 cloves garlic, minced
1 deli rotisserie chicken, diced
   and bones discarded
2 32-oz. containers low-sodium
   vegetable or chicken broth

14-1/2 oz. can diced tomatoes
9-oz. pkg. refrigerated cheese
   tortellini, uncooked
3 c. baby spinach
salt and pepper to taste
Garnish: grated Parmesan cheese

In a large soup pot, heat oil over medium-high heat. Add onion and carrot; cook for about 5 to 6 minutes, until beginning to soften. Add garlic and cook, stirring often, for about one minute. Mix in chicken, broth and diced tomatoes with juice. Bring to a boil; reduce heat to medium Add tortellini and cook for about 8 minutes. Add the spinach; cook for one to 2 minutes, until wilted. Remove from heat; season with salt and pepper. Serve topped with Parmesan cheese. Serves 6.

Soup is extra tasty served up in toasty bread bowls. Slice the tops off small round loaves of bread and hollow out. Brush the insides with olive oil...sprinkle with Italian seasoning and grated Parmesan cheese, if you like. Bake at 350 degrees for about 10 minutes.

Back-to-School
FALL RECIPES

Italian Sausage & Spinach Soup
Julie Gunn
Watervliet, MI

I make this hearty soup for my family and they love it...perfect for a chilly autumn day! Serve with warm Italian bread or rolls.

4 lbs. potatoes, peeled and cubed
2 to 3 cubes chicken bouillon
2 lbs. Italian pork sausage links,
  casings removed
1 lb. sliced mushrooms
1 c. onion, chopped

2 12-oz. pkgs. chopped spinach,
  thawed and drained
1 T. Italian seasoning
pepper to taste
32-oz. container whipping cream

In a saucepan, cover potatoes with water; add bouillon cubes. Bring to a boil over high heat. Cook until potatoes are tender, 15 to 20 minutes; drain. Meanwhile, in a soup pot over medium heat, brown sausage with mushrooms and onion; drain. Add potatoes, spinach, seasonings and cream; cook over medium-low heat until spinach is wilted. Makes 8 servings.

Cheese-Topped Biscuits
Sharon Crider
Junction City, KS

A quick, tasty way to dress up refrigerator biscuits!

2 7-1/2 oz. tubes refrigerated
  biscuits, divided
1 c. shredded Cheddar cheese

2 T. light cream
1/2 t. poppy seed
1/8 t. dry mustard

Arrange 15 biscuits, overlapping, around the edge of a greased, aluminum foil-lined 9" round cake pan. Arrange remaining biscuits in the center. Combine remaining ingredients in a bowl; spread evenly over biscuits. Bake at 425 degrees for 15 minutes, or until golden. Serve warm. Makes 20 biscuits.

For a quick warm-you-up cup of potato soup, whisk leftover mashed potatoes into hot chicken broth.

Chilly-Day
SOUPS & BREADS

Beef Barley Soup

Barbara Klein
Newburgh, IN

The perfect soup for a cold day...just add some hearty country-style bread and butter. Long simmering makes it delicious.

1 lb. stew beef cubes
2 beef soup bones
1/2 onion, chopped
8 c. water
14-1/2 oz. can diced tomatoes

4 stalks celery, diced
2 carrots, peeled and diced
3 cubes beef bouillon
1/2 c. instant barley, uncooked

In a large soup pot, combine beef cubes, beef bones, onion and water. Bring to a boil over high heat; reduce heat to medium-low and cook until beef is tender, about 2 hours. Remove meat from bones and if necessary, cut beef cubes in half; return beef to pot. Add tomatoes with juice, vegetables and bouillon cubes; simmer over low heat for one hour. Stir in barley and simmer for 30 minutes, or until barley is tender. Makes 8 servings.

For many years every fall, I hosted a Halloween party for my co-workers and their families in a local park pavilion. Of course, we all wore costumes, and there were games for the children. Thanks to some donations, I was able to hire a deejay to play the music, and there was even a disco ball. The best part of the evening, though, was the "chili dump." Everyone brought a pot of their own chili, and it all went into one big kettle.
What great chili we all made together!

– Sue Klapper, Muskego, WI

Minestrone Soup

Panda Spurgin
Bella Vista, AR

This soup tastes like you worked all day preparing it, and the house smells wonderful! Serve with crusty bread.

2 15-1/2 oz. cans red kidney
   beans
14-1/2 oz. can diced tomatoes
2-1/2 c. water
2 T. dried parsley
1/2 t. pepper
2 cloves garlic, pressed
1 to 2 zucchini, cubed
1 to 2 carrots, peeled and diced

1/2 c. celery, chopped
2 green onions, chopped
3 T. butter
1 T. olive oil
1/4 c. elbow macaroni, uncooked
1/2 c. dry white wine or water
2 T. pesto sauce
Garnish: shredded Parmesan
   cheese

Add undrained beans to a large soup pot. With a fork, mash about 2/3 of beans. Add tomatoes with juice, water, seasonings, garlic, vegetables, butter and oil. Bring to a boil over high heat; reduce heat to medium-low and simmer for one hour. Stir in macaroni, wine or water and pesto. Simmer for about another 15 minutes, until macaroni is tender. Makes 6 to 8 servings.

When fixing sandwiches for lunchboxes, first spread a light layer of softened butter on the bread. The butter keeps the bread from absorbing the moisture from the filling and becoming soggy.

Chilly-Day
SOUPS & BREADS

Sassy Black Bean Soup

Regina Wickline
Pebble Beach, CA

This yummy soup is ready in a jiffy! I like to garnish the bowls of soup with sliced avocado, sour cream and a sprinkle of cilantro.

1 T. olive oil
1 c. onion, chopped
2 cloves garlic, minced
14-1/2 oz. can petite diced
   tomatoes
2 16-oz. cans black beans,
   drained and rinsed

10-1/2 oz. can chicken broth
1/2 c. picante sauce
1/4 c. water
1 t. ground cumin
1 T. lime juice

Heat oil in a large saucepan over medium heat. Add onion and garlic; sauté until tender. Stir in tomatoes with juice and remaining ingredients except lime juice. Bring to a boil; reduce heat to medium-low. Simmer for 15 minutes, stirring occasionally. Just before serving, stir in lime juice. Serves 4.

Vintage tea towels are perfect for lining bread baskets. They'll keep freshly baked rolls toasty warm and add a dash of color to the table. Look for fun designs like farm animals or happy flowers that will tickle the kids.

Back-to-School
FALL RECIPES

Country Chicken Stew

Karen Ensign
Providence, UT

A very flavorful stew for a chilly day! Make some homemade biscuits while it simmers, for a wonderful meal.

4 slices bacon
2 lbs. boneless, skinless chicken
   thighs, cubed
Optional: 2 T. canola oil
4 carrots, peeled and cut into
   1/2-inch pieces
1 onion, diced
1 stalk celery, minced
2 cloves garlic, minced
5 c. no-salt chicken broth,
   divided

1/2 c. sherry or chicken broth
2 t. Worcestershire sauce
3 T. butter, sliced
1/3 c. all-purpose flour
12-oz. can evaporated milk
1/2 t. dried thyme
1/2 t. smoked paprika
1 t. kosher salt
1 t. pepper
1 lb. potatoes, peeled and cubed
Garnish: chopped fresh parsley

In a Dutch oven over medium heat, cook bacon until crisp. Transfer bacon to a bowl, reserving drippings in pan. Working in small batches, cook chicken in drippings over medium-high heat until golden on all sides. Add oil, if needed. Transfer chicken to a large bowl. Reduce heat to medium. Add carrots, onion and celery; cook until softened. Add garlic; cook for 30 seconds, or until fragrant. Turn heat to medium-high. Add one cup chicken broth, sherry or broth and Worcestershire sauce; scrape up any brown bits from the bottom of pan. Bring to a boil, stirring occasionally, for about 10 minutes, until liquid is reduced and vegetables start to sizzle. Add butter; stir to melt. Sprinkle flour over vegetables. Gradually stir in remaining broth, evaporated milk and seasonings; whisk until smooth. Add chicken and potatoes; bring to a low boil. Cook until chicken and vegetables are fork-tender, about 20 minutes, stirring occasionally. Garnish servings with crumbled bacon and parsley. Makes 8 servings.

To give a nutritious boost to recipes, add finely minced veggies
to your family's favorite soups...they'll hardly be noticed.

Chilly-Day
SOUPS & BREADS

Easy Pan Biscuits

Diana Chaney
Olathe, KS

*The perfect go-with for homemade soup. You'll love how simple
these biscuits are to make...the kids can help roll the dough.
Serve with butter and honey or jam.*

2 c. biscuit baking mix
1/2 c. sour cream
6 T. lemon-lime soda
2 t. dried parsley

1 t. dried basil
1/4 t. coarse pepper
3 T. butter, melted and divided

In a bowl, combine all ingredients except butter. Mix with a fork until a
soft dough forms. With floured hands, divide dough in half; divide each
half into 10 portions and shape into balls. Place biscuits in a greased
8" round cake pan, with sides of biscuits touching. Brush with half of
melted butter. Bake at 425 degrees for 15 minutes, or until golden.
Brush with remaining melted butter; serve immediately. Makes
20 biscuits.

Hang an old-fashioned peg rack inside the back door,
then hang up all the kids' backpacks plus a tote bag for
yourself. No more mad rush every morning!

Back-to-School
FALL RECIPES

Chicken Taco Soup

Shawna Jimenez
Spring Valley, CA

I love this slow-cooker soup...it's warming and always hits the spot. It is perfect for those rainy or snowy days. It's super kid-friendly and a party in your mouth!

15-1/2 oz. can hot chili beans
15-1/2 oz. can regular chili beans
1-1/2 c. frozen corn
2 c. frozen green or red pepper strips
2 4-oz. cans diced green chiles
1 c. onion, chopped
1-oz. pkg. mild taco seasoning mix

1-oz. pkg. jalapeño & onion taco seasoning mix
1 c. water
Optional: 1 t. red pepper flakes
4 boneless, skinless chicken breasts
Garnish: shredded cheese, sour cream, avocado slices, tortilla strips, black olives

In a 6-quart slow cooker, combine undrained beans and remaining ingredients except chicken and garnish. Stir until well combined. Place chicken on top, pushing it down slightly into the soup mixture. Cover and cook on low setting for 6 to 8 hours, until chicken is very tender. Shred chicken; stir into soup. Garnish with desired toppings. Makes 6 to 8 servings.

With school and after-school activities, dinner can be a challenge. Now's the time to get out that slow cooker! Other than a quick chop of a few ingredients, recipes are usually a simple matter of tossing everything into the pot.

Chilly-Day
SOUPS & BREADS

Tuscan Soup

Andrea Czarniecki
Northville, MI

This is comfort in a bowl. When I came home from the hospital after having surgery, a good friend of mine brought me a pot of this wonderful soup. It has become a family favorite. The whole house smells wonderful as it cooks and it is so impressive when served. I like to make it for anyone I want to show love to.

10 to 12 new redskin potatoes, cubed
4 to 6 c. chicken broth
1 lb. ground mild Italian pork sausage
1 c. onion, chopped
3 cloves garlic, minced

1 to 2 t. fresh basil, snipped
1 T. butter
1 c. milk
2 c. fresh spinach or kale, torn
Garnish: shredded Parmesan cheese

Place potatoes in a large soup pot; add enough broth to cover potatoes. Bring to a boil over high heat. Reduce heat to medium; cook for 18 to 20 minutes, until potatoes are soft. Do not drain. Meanwhile, in a skillet over medium heat, cook sausage, onion and garlic until sausage is browned; drain and crumble sausage. Add sausage mixture and basil to potato mixture; simmer for 20 to 30 minutes. Add butter and milk; stir until melted and creamy. Add spinach or kale; cook for a few more minutes, until wilted. Serve topped with Parmesan cheese. Serves 4.

Need a quick snack for the kids? Serve up an old favorite, Ants on a Log...celery sticks filled with peanut butter and sprinkled with raisins. Kids love it!

Back-to-School
FALL RECIPES

Busy-Day, Lazy-Day Bean Soup

Dianne Young
Salt Lake City, UT

I always have these ingredients on hand, so whenever the family stops by and I need a quick dinner, I can fix this recipe in minutes.

1-1/2 lbs. ground beef
1 c. onion, diced
28-oz. can whole tomatoes
28-oz. can pork & beans
2 10-3/4 oz. cans minestrone
  soup

2 T. brown sugar, packed
1 t. dried oregano
salt and pepper to taste

Brown beef with onion in a skillet over medium heat. Drain and transfer to a 4-quart slow cooker. Add undrained tomatoes and beans, soup, brown sugar and seasonings. Cover and cook on low setting for 3 to 4 hours, until hot and bubbly. Serves 6.

Ann's Sweet Cornbread

Ann Davis
Brookville, IN

If your family likes cornbread, they'll love this one!
Serve with plenty of butter.

1 c. all-purpose flour
3/4 c. cornmeal
2/3 c. sugar
3-1/2 t. baking powder
1/4 t. salt

1 egg, beaten
1 c. milk
1/4 c. oil
2-1/2 T. honey

In a large bowl, stir together flour, cornmeal, sugar, baking powder and salt. In a small bowl, stir together egg, milk, oil and honey. Add egg mixture to flour mixture; beat thoroughly. Pour batter into a greased 8"x8" baking pan. Bake at 400 degrees for 20 to 24 minutes. Cut into squares. Makes 8 to 10 servings.

What we learn with pleasure we never forget.
– Alfred Mercier

44

Chilly-Day
SOUPS & BREADS

Cream of Bacon & Tomato Soup

Janis Parr
Ontario, Canada

This special tomato soup is so delicious with the rich taste
of bacon and onion. The kids love it!

4 slices bacon, cut up	1 t. sugar
4 slices onion, diced	1 t. salt
2-2/3 T. all-purpose flour	1/4 t. pepper
2 c. tomatoes, chopped and	1 bay leaf
mashed	2 c. whole milk

In a saucepan over medium heat, cook bacon until crisp. Drain,
reserving drippings in pan. Add onion to drippings; cook until soft.
Sprinkle flour over onion; stir until smooth. Reduce heat to low, Add
tomatoes all at once; stir until well blended. Add sugar and seasonings;
cook for a few minutes longer. Discard bay leaf. Add milk; heat through
without boiling. Makes 4 servings.

Crazy Crackers

Sophia Collins
McHenry, MS

This recipe was given to me by a co-worker, and these crackers have
become a staple at every celebration. Serve alongside soup, sliced
cheese, cheese balls or any kind of dip.

4 sleeves saltine crackers	2 c. canola oil
1-oz. pkg. ranch salad dressing	1 to 3 t. red pepper flakes,
mix	to taste

Transfer crackers to a one-gallon plastic zipping bag. In a bowl, mix
remaining ingredients; pour over crackers. Seal bag and turn to coat. Let
stand at room temperature overnight, if possible, turning bag over about
once every hour. Makes 25 servings.

Make bean soups thick & creamy. Purée a cup or so of the soup
in a blender and stir it back into the soup pot.

Back-to-School
FALL RECIPES

Turkey Noodle Soup

Wendy Jo Minotte
Duluth, MN

*This is a delicious way to use leftover Thanksgiving turkey.
If you don't have 3 quarts turkey broth, use water and
soup base to make up the difference.*

16-oz. pkg. thin egg noodles,
   uncooked
3 qts. turkey broth
1 lb. carrots, peeled and diced
4 stalks celery, diced

1/2 c. onion, diced
2 c. cooked turkey, diced
Optional: 1 T. turkey soup base,
   or to taste

Cook noodles according to package directions; drain and set aside.
Meanwhile, in a separate stockpot, bring broth to a simmer over
medium heat. Add carrots, celery and onion; simmer for about
10 minutes, until tender. Stir in cooked noodles, turkey and soup
base, if using; simmer just until heated through. Makes 6 servings.

Serving soup to little eaters? Cut out Jack-o'-Lantern faces
from cheese slices. Top servings of soup with the
cut-out shapes. How fun!

Chilly-Day
SOUPS & BREADS

Hearty Turkey-Vegetable Soup

JoAnn
Gooseberry Patch

A soup to warm you on a crisp autumn day. You'll be thankful you had leftovers!

2 T. oil
1/2 c. onion, diced
2 cloves garlic, minced
8 c. turkey or chicken broth
3 c. cooked turkey, diced
1/2 c. carrot, peeled and diced
1/2 c. celery, diced
1 to 2 potatoes, peeled and diced

1/2 c. quick-cooking barley, uncooked
2 c. cooked green beans, corn, broccoli or other vegetables, chopped
1 T. dried parsley
1 t. dried marjoram
salt and pepper to taste

Heat oil in a large stockpot over medium heat. Add onion and garlic; sauté for 3 to 4 minutes. Add broth and bring to a boil; reduce heat to medium-low. Stir in remaining ingredients. Cover and simmer gently for 35 to 40 minutes, until potatoes and barley are tender. Makes 6 to 8 servings.

Get the new school year off to a great start! Set up a homework caddy filled with pencils, crayons, markers and all the other supplies kids will need...no more excuses! Check the kitchenware aisle at the grocery store for plastic caddies in bright colors.

Back-to-School
FALL RECIPES

Vegetable Soup for a Crowd

Kelly Alderson
Erie, PA

My family enjoys this veggie-packed soup...it's a tasty warmer-upper alongside grilled cheese sandwiches. I check the fridge, the freezer and even the last of the garden for vegetables to use up.

2 T. olive oil
2 c. onions, chopped
1 c. celery, thinly sliced
2 t. Italian seasoning
salt and pepper to taste
3 14-1/2 oz. cans reduced-
   sodium vegetable or chicken
   broth

3 c. water
28-oz. can petite diced tomatoes
1 T. tomato paste
8 c. assorted fresh or frozen
   vegetables like potatoes,
   carrots, zucchini, corn, green
   beans, lima beans and peas,
   chopped

Heat oil in a large stockpot over medium heat. Add onions, celery and seasonings. Cook, stirring often, until onions are translucent, 5 to 8 minutes. Add broth, water, tomatoes with juice and tomato paste; bring to a boil. Reduce heat to medium-low; simmer for 20 minutes. Add assorted vegetables; return to a simmer. Cook, uncovered, until vegetables are tender, 20 to 25 minutes. Season with more salt and pepper, if desired. Serves 8 to 10.

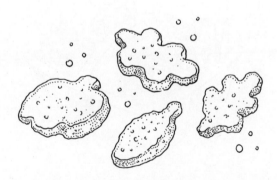

Cute soup croutons! Butter bread slices and cut into shapes
using mini cookie cutters. Bake at 200 degrees for about
10 minutes, until crunchy and golden.

Chilly-Day
SOUPS & BREADS

Vegetable Beef Soup

Diane Cohen
Breinigsville, PE

I make this simple soup often in the fall and winter.

1 lb. ground beef, browned
 and drained
2 c. tomato juice

2 c. beef broth
16-oz. pkg. frozen mixed
 vegetables

Combine all ingredients in a slow cooker. Cover and cook on high setting for 3 hours; turn to low setting and cook an additional 3 to 4 hours. Makes 4 to 6 servings.

Pimento Corn Muffins

Patti Sherman Jones
Vero Beach, FL

Whenever I take these muffins to church suppers, I am always asked to bring them again the next time!

8-1/2 oz. pkg. corn muffin mix
1 egg, beaten
1/3 c. milk

1/4 t. chili powder
7-oz. jar sliced pimentos, drained
 and chopped

In a bowl, combine all ingredients except pimentos; stir to mix well. Fold in pimentos; let stand for 3 to 4 minutes. Fill 8 paper-lined muffin cups with batter, 2/3 full. Bake at 400 degrees for 20 to 25 minutes, watching to avoid browning. Makes 8 muffins.

A baker's secret! Grease muffin cups on the bottoms and just halfway up the sides...the muffins will bake up nicely puffed on top.

Back-to-School
FALL RECIPES

Country Soup Supper

Vickie
Gooseberry Patch

*Hearty enough to stand alone, this soup is comforting with
extraordinary flavor...perfect on a windy fall day.*

3 whole cloves
1 small yellow onion, peeled
5 15-1/2 oz. cans Great Northern
    beans, drained and rinsed
6 c. water
3 smoked ham hocks, or
    1/2 lb. cooked ham, diced
2 c. potatoes, peeled and cubed
1-1/2 c. sweet onion, chopped

2/3 c. celery, chopped
2/3 c. carrot, peeled and sliced
1/2 t. dried thyme
1 t. dried parsley
1 bay leaf
1 t. salt
3/4 t. pepper
Optional: 2 T. fresh parsley,
    chopped

Press cloves into whole onion; set aside. In a large stockpot, combine remaining ingredients except optional parsley; add onion with cloves. Bring to a boil over high heat; reduce heat to medium-low. Cover and simmer for 45 minutes, stirring occasionally. Discard bay leaf and onion with cloves. Remove ham hocks, if using; dice meat and return to soup. Stir in parsley, if desired. Makes 10 to 12 servings.

Try something new for brown bag lunches...roll any combination of cheese, deli meat and veggies in a tortilla. Even a peanut butter & jelly wrap tastes terrific!

Chilly-Day
SOUPS & BREADS

Parmesan Bread Sticks

Amanda Porter
North Ogden, UT

These are great alongside hot soup or your favorite pasta dish.

1 T. instant dry yeast
2 T. sugar
1/2 t. salt
1-1/2 c. very warm water,
   about 110 to 115 degrees

3 c. all-purpose flour
2 to 4 T. butter, melted
grated Parmesan cheese and
   garlic salt to taste

In a large bowl, dissolve yeast, sugar and salt in warm water. Add flour; stir for 3 minutes. Let dough rest for 10 minutes. On a floured surface, roll dough out to about 12 inches by 8 inches. Cut into strips 1/2-inch wide. Place on a lightly greased baking sheet. Brush with melted butter. Sprinkle with Parmesan cheese and garlic salt. Let rise 10 minutes. Bake at 400 degrees for about 10 minutes, until lightly golden. Makes about 1-1/2 dozen.

Back in the late 40s and early 50s, our next-door neighbor had three very large sycamore trees that grew in a line between her house and ours. Every autumn, all the leaves would fall, leaving a thick layer of leaves that my father had to rake up. In those days, we could rake them into piles near the street and then burn them. As piles of leaves burned throughout the neighborhood, kids would run and hop over the piles, something I would never let my kids or grandkids do these days! We would smell like smoke for days, even after bathing. I still miss that smell!

– Judy Petersen, Fresno, CA

Back-to-School
FALL RECIPES

Easiest Beef Stew

Christine Dunham
Bangor, ME

This is the best and easiest slow-cooker stew recipe...
it turns out delicious every time!

1 lb. stew beef cubes
14-1/2 oz. can stewed tomatoes
10-1/2 oz. can golden mushroom
  soup
4 to 6 potatoes, quartered
2 cloves garlic, pressed

4 onions, quartered
4 carrots, peeled and quartered
4 stalks celery, cut up
1 to 2 bay leaves
Optional: 1 small turnip, peeled
  and cut up

Add all ingredients to a 5-quart slow cooker; do not add any water.
Cover and cook on low setting for 6 to 8 hours, until beef and
vegetables are tender. Discard bay leaves before serving. Makes 6 to
8 servings.

Pitch a tent in the backyard on a fall night so the kids can
camp out, tell ghost stories and play flashlight tag.
What a great way to make memories!

Chilly-Day
SOUPS & BREADS

Constance's Cabbage Soup

Constance Bockstoce
Dallas, GA

Ever since I was a young child...over 60 years ago!...I have eaten this soup for dinner on cold evenings. It has been a favorite for my children and my grandchildren. Tastes great the next day, too.

32-oz. container chicken broth
1/2 to 1 head cabbage, cut into
   large cubes
2 lbs. baby carrots, cut in half
1 lb. smoked pork sausage link,
   sliced 1/2-inch thick

2 lbs. potatoes, peeled and cut
   into large cubes
2 T. onion, finely chopped
1 t. pepper, or to taste
Optional: 1 t. dried basil

Layer ingredients in a large stockpot in the order listed. Bring to a boil over medium-high heat. Turn down heat to medium-low. Cover and simmer for one hour, or until vegetables are tender, stirring occasionally. Makes 6 to 8 servings.

Pumpkin Spice Muffins

Charlotte Smith
Alexandria, PA

I found this recipe among my mother's handwritten recipes. I gave it a try, and believe me, you just can't stop at one!

18-1/4 oz. pkg. spice cake mix
15-oz. can pumpkin
3 eggs, beaten

1/3 c. oil
1/3 c. water

In a bowl, beat all ingredients together. Pour batter into greased or paper-lined muffin cups, filling 2/3 full. Bake at 350 degrees for 20 minutes, or until golden. Makes 2 dozen.

On chilly nights, put on your jammies, wrap up in a quilt and eat soup by the fire!

Back-to-School
FALL RECIPES

Italian Chicken Vegetable Soup
Beverley Williams
San Antonio, TX

My family loves this slow-cooker soup on chilly days in fall and winter.

2 c. cooked chicken, cubed
3 c. chicken broth
1 carrot, peeled and sliced
1 tomato, diced
1 small bunch fresh spinach, chopped
12 fresh green beans, broken into one-inch pieces
1 zucchini, cubed

4 mushrooms, sliced
1 T. onion, minced
2 T. fresh basil, snipped
1 t. dried oregano
1/2 t. garlic powder
8-oz. can tomato sauce
1 c. small shell or elbow macaroni, uncooked

Combine all ingredients in a 4-quart slow cooker. Cover and cook on high setting for 2 to 3 hours, until vegetables are tender. Add more broth or water, if needed. Makes 6 servings.

Transfer leftover soup into smaller containers
before refrigerating or freezing...easy to microwave
later for a quick lunch!

Chilly-Day
SOUPS & BREADS

Meatball & Tortellini Soup

Kathy Courington
Canton, GA

I had never fixed meatballs this way and wanted to try something different. My husband said this slow-cooker recipe was a keeper! Very warming-to-the-tummy goodness.

25-oz. pkg. frozen meatballs
2 14-1/2 oz. cans stewed
   tomatoes
32-oz. container beef or
   vegetable broth
1 onion, chopped

2 T. Italian seasoning
2 t. garlic, minced
16-oz. pkg. refrigerated cheese
   tortellini, uncooked
Garnish: shredded Parmesan and
   mozzarella cheeses

Place frozen meatballs in a 5-quart slow cooker. Add tomatoes with juice, broth, onion, seasoning and garlic. Cover and cook on low setting for 6 hours, or on high setting for 4 hours. During the last hour, add tortellini to slow cooker. Serve topped with cheeses. Makes 4 to 6 servings.

Freshen up a thermos or sports bottle in a jiffy. Spoon in a heaping teaspoon of baking soda, then fill with boiling water. Cap, shake gently and rinse...all ready to use again!

Back-to-School
FALL RECIPES

Mexicano Chili

LaShelle Brown
Mulvane, KS

We serve this chili at all of our fall gatherings...and there is never any left at the end of the evening! Add a basket of saltine crackers and some shredded cheese for the perfect meal for sharing.

4 lbs. lean ground beef
1/3 c. all-purpose flour
2 t. garlic, minced
3 to 4 T. chili powder
1 T. ground cumin

2 t. salt
1/2 t. pepper
46-oz. can tomato juice
1 to 2 15-1/2 oz. cans kidney
   beans, drained and rinsed

Working in batches, brown beef in a large skillet over medium heat until no longer pink. Drain; transfer to a 6-quart slow cooker. Sprinkle with flour, garlic and seasonings; stir to combine evenly. Add tomato juice and stir. Cover and cook on low setting for 6 to 8 hours. Stir in kidney beans one to 2 hours before done. Serves 12 to 14.

Looking for a new no-mess way to decorate Jack-o'-Lanterns? Try duct tape! It comes in lots of fun colors and is super-easy to cut into shapes...great for kids to craft with. Later, the uncut pumpkin can even be re-purposed for pies, if you wish.

Chilly-Day
SOUPS & BREADS

Apple Corn Muffins

Jill Burton
Gooseberry Patch

These yummy muffins go with just about any autumn meal!

2 8-1/2 oz. pkgs. corn muffin
  mix
2 eggs, beaten
1/2 c. milk
2 McIntosh apples, peeled,
  cored and grated

3 T. sugar, divided
1 t. apple pie spice
Optional: 1/2 c. chopped
  walnuts

In a large bowl, combine muffin mixes, eggs, milk, apple, 2 tablespoons sugar and spice. Stir just until moistened. Spoon 1/3 cup batter into each of 12 lightly greased muffin cups. Sprinkle with remaining sugar and walnuts, if using. Bake at 400 degrees for 18 to 20 minutes. Makes one dozen.

When the air gets a chill, we open our freezer! All summer long, fresh veggies, as well as leftover pieces of bread, muffins and doughnuts, are put into the freezer. When the air gets that first fall chill, we open the freezer and cook up a wonderful "everything-but-the-kitchen-sink" soup and a yummy bread pudding. My husband and I have done this for 25 years. It signals to us the end of summer and the beginning of soup and sweater season!
– Lisanne Miller, Wells, ME

Back-to-School
FALL RECIPES

Stone Soup

Diane Himpelmann
Ringwood, IL

When I taught school, my class and I cooked together at least once per month. One day we would make vegetable soup, based on the old children's storybook of Stone Soup. Each child brought a vegetable to class, which they would peel and I would chop. We added these to the broth, and enjoyed eating the soup together. This was a favorite activity in our classroom.

assorted vegetables, peeled and
  chopped or sliced
1 onion, chopped
vegetable or chicken broth

Optional: 1/2 c. alphabet
  macaroni, uncooked
1 large smooth stone, well
  washed

Combine vegetables and onion in an electric skillet; add enough broth to cover vegetables. Stir in macaroni, if using; add the stone. Cook over medium to medium-high heat for 20 to 30 minutes, until vegetables are tender. Once the vegetables are done, soup is served! The student who finds the stone in his or her soup bowl becomes the "student of the day." You can use a meatball if you are concerned about the stone, but I never had a problem. Kids love it! The number of servings will depend on the amount of vegetables and broth used.

A serrated plastic knife is perfect for beginning cooks helping out with the Stone Soup or other favorite dishes. They'll be able to practice cutting ingredients safely, with all fingers kept above the blade.

Kid-Friendly
VEGGIE
DISHES

Back-to-School
FALL RECIPES

Bowtie Picnic Pasta Salad

Michelle Papp
Rutherford, NJ

This pasta salad is easy and great for any backyard picnic or casual meal. It's a delicious side for burgers, hot dogs or grilled chicken.

8-oz. pkg. bowtie pasta,
  uncooked
1 ear sweet corn, husks removed
1 carrot, peeled and diced
1 stalk celery, diced
1/2 t. paprika

salt and pepper to taste
1 c. mayonnaise
1/2 c. sour cream
1 t. Dijon mustard
Garnish: additional paprika

Cook pasta according to package directions, just until tender; drain and rinse with cold water. Meanwhile, add ear of corn to a saucepan of boiling water. Cook for 5 minutes; drain and let cool. Slice kernels from cob and set aside. In a large bowl, combine pasta, corn, carrot and celery. Toss lightly; season with paprika, salt and pepper. In a small bowl, combine mayonnaise, sour cream and mustard. Pour over salad; toss to coat. Sprinkle with a little more paprika for color. Cover and chill for one hour before serving. Makes 6 servings.

For picnics, a wheelbarrow or wagon is just right for holding paper plates and cups along with flatware and napkins. It's easy to take right to the picnic spot and keeps picnic tables free for holding all the scrumptious food!

Kid-Friendly
VEGGIE DISHES

Cauliflower Salad

Nannette Scarborough
Farmerville, LA

My kids loved this chilled salad...it was a great way to get them to eat cauliflower! Always a sure bet.

1 head cauliflower, chopped
1 green pepper, chopped
1 tomato, chopped
1/2 onion, chopped
1/4 c. Italian salad dressing

1 c. mayonnaise-style salad
   dressing
1 t. salt
1 t. pepper, or more to taste

In a large bowl, combine all vegetables; set aside. In a small bowl, mix salad dressings and seasonings. Pour over vegetables; toss to coat well. Cover and refrigerate at least one hour. Serves 12.

Broccoli-Raisin Salad

Carolyn Deckard
Bedford, IN

This salad was served at the lunchroom where I used to work. Whenever they had it on the menu, I would always have it for lunch that day. It's my favorite salad, and so easy to fix.

2 to 3 c. broccoli, chopped
5 slices bacon, crisply cooked
   and crumbled
1 red onion, diced

1/2 c. mayonnaise
1/2 c. raisins
1/4 c. sugar
1 T. vinegar

Combine broccoli, bacon and onion in a bowl. Combine remaining ingredients in a separate bowl; cover both bowls and refrigerate overnight. At serving time, drizzle mayonnaise mixture over broccoli mixture; toss to coat well and serve. Makes 4 servings.

Kids are more likely to eat salads if veggies are cut into bite-size pieces that are easy to eat. A mix of crunchy textures (never soggy!) and bright colors is sure to appeal.

Back-to-School
FALL RECIPES

Salad on a Stick

Janis Parr
Ontario, Canada

This is a delicious and nutritious salad you can eat with your hands. A tasty and fun way to eat your veggies!

8 small new potatoes
8 small white mushrooms
8 pearl onions
1 yellow pepper, cut into
   one-inch squares
1 red pepper, cut into one-inch
   squares

16 cherry tomatoes
1 zucchini, sliced 1/4-inch thick
8 long wooden skewers
salt and pepper to taste
red wine vinaigrette salad
   dressing to taste

In a saucepan over medium heat, cook potatoes in boiling water for 5 to 8 minutes. Add mushrooms and onions to saucepan; continue cooking for 5 more minutes, or until potatoes are tender. Drain and cool. Thread all vegetables alternately onto 8 skewers; sprinkle with salt and pepper. Place skewers in a large shallow dish and drizzle with salad dressing. Cover and refrigerate for at least 2 hours, turning several times to coat with dressing. Makes 8 servings.

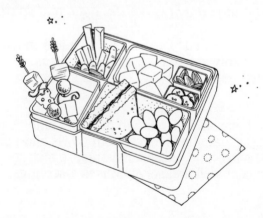

Finger foods make lunchtime more fun! Fill the compartments of a sectioned container with a variety of your kids' favorite finger foods...cubes of deli turkey and cheese, animal crackers, baby carrots and ranch dressing. They're sure to help you think of plenty more!

Kid-Friendly VEGGIE DISHES

Sweet Carrot Salad

Jessica Silva
East Berlin, CT

This carrot salad actually tastes better the next day! It's a fun, sweet salad for picnics and lunchboxes anytime.

2-1/2 c. carrots, peeled and
  shredded
1/2 Granny Smith apple, cored
  and thinly sliced
1 stalk celery, thinly sliced

1/2 c. raisins
1/2 c. mayonnaise
2 t. lemon juice
2 t. cinnamon
1 t. nutmeg

Combine carrots, apple, celery and raisins in a bowl. Add mayonnaise; stir until well coated. Add lemon juice; stir well. Stir in spices; cover and chill until serving time. Makes 8 to 10 servings.

Autumn has always been my favorite time of the year. Because my birthday falls around Halloween, my sweet mother indulged my desire to build a "Haunted House" in our front yard. She took me downtown to the Army-Navy surplus store, where I was allowed to pick out the largest parachute I could find. Once home, my friends and I would stake it up. I'd sneak into the attic to find Christmas lights that were strategically strung around the "house." Then we dressed into our scariest costumes and took our places. We would charge a whole penny to those in the neighborhood who dared enter in! What fun we had, practicing our best werewolf howls and most frightening witch cackles!

– Kathy Neuppert Swanson, Hemet, CA

Back-to-School
FALL RECIPES

Pepperoni Pizza Pasta Salad

Mia Rossi
Charlotte, NC

This fun salad has everyone's favorite pizza flavors!
Perfect for tailgating parties.

3 c. bowtie pasta, uncooked
6-oz. pkg. mozzarella cheese,
 cubed
4-oz. pkg. mini pepperoni slices
2 c. roma tomatoes, diced
1 c. green pepper, diced

3/4 c. sliced black olives, drained
1/2 c. Italian salad dressing
1/4 t. pepper
Garnish: shredded Parmesan
 cheese

Cook pasta according to package directions, just until tender; drain and
rinse with cold water. Meanwhile, in a large bowl, mix remaining
ingredients except Parmesan cheese. Add pasta; toss to combine. Cover
and refrigerate for about 2 hours, until chilled. Serve topped with grated
Parmesan cheese. Makes 8 servings.

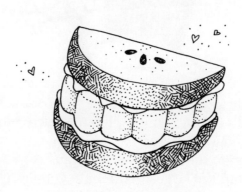

Make "apple smiles" with your little ones! Cut apples into
8 wedges. Spread peanut butter on one side of each slice. Place
mini marshmallows on the peanut butter for teeth. Place another
peanut-buttered apple slice on top so the peel sides match and
the marshmallows are sandwiched between apples.

Kid-Friendly VEGGIE DISHES

Fresh Cucumber Salad

Carrie Kelderman
Pella, IA

I have fond garden memories of when I was seven years old. Mom would let me pick cucumbers fresh from our garden, and would let me wash them and cut them up with a plastic knife. She'd help me put the rest of this salad together. Now, I am teaching my own seven-year-old daughter the same thing. We love our garden and kitchen time spent together with three generations!

2 cucumbers, halved, seeds
   removed and cubed
1 to 2 tomatoes, cubed
3/4 c. red onion, cut into
   thin strips

3 T. olive oil
3 T. white vinegar
3 T. sugar or sugar substitute
salt and pepper to taste

In a large bowl, mix together cucumbers, tomatoes and onion. In a small bowl, whisk together remaining ingredients. Drizzle oil mixture over cucumber mixture; toss to coat well. Cover and refrigerate for at least 2 hours before serving. Makes 4 to 6 servings.

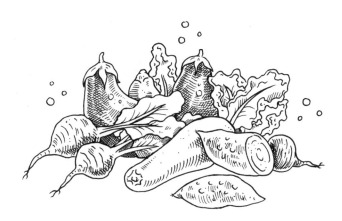

Tempt young appetites with veggies in a rainbow of colors...
red beets, orange sweet potatoes, yellow summer squash, dark
green kale and purple eggplant. Fill their plates and eat up!

Back-to-School
FALL RECIPES

Easy Potato Salad

Lynnette Jones
East Flat Rock, NC

Doesn't everyone want potato salad at a potluck? This one has a hint of onion, but it won't overwhelm your taste buds.

3 lbs. white potatoes, peeled
   and cubed
1-1/2 T. salt
1 c. mayonnaise

1/4 c. celery, finely chopped
1 t. onion, finely chopped
1 t. celery seed

Add potatoes and salt to a saucepan; cover with water. Bring to a boil over high heat; cook for 7 minutes, or until fork-tender. Drain potatoes in a colander for 10 to 20 minutes. Meanwhile, combine remaining ingredients in a large bowl; mix well. Add potatoes and toss to coat. Chill. Makes 8 to 10 servings.

Family Pasta Salad

Tiffany Jones
Batesville, AR

This pasta has been served at every family get-together since I was a child. It is quick, easy and best of all...yummy!

12-oz. pkg. bowtie pasta,
   uncooked
14-1/2 oz. can diced tomatoes
   with green chiles

1 cucumber, chopped
8-oz. bottle Italian salad
   dressing

Cook pasta according to package directions, just until tender; drain and rinse with cold water. Place pasta in a large bowl with a lid; add remaining ingredients. Put lid on bowl; shake bowl well to mix. Refrigerate, covered, until chilled. Serves 6.

The best way to make children good is to make them happy.
– Oscar Wilde

Kid-Friendly
VEGGIE DISHES

Lisa's Linguine Salad

Eleanor Dionne
Beverly, MA

This is one of my daughter's special salads. She makes it on request for every get-together. We enjoy it with linguine, but rotini or penne pasta works well too.

16-oz. pkg. linguine pasta,
  uncooked
1 tomato, diced
1 cucumber, diced

1 red onion, diced
8-oz. bottle Italian salad dressing
2 to 3 T. salad supreme
  seasoning

Cook pasta according to package directions; drain and rinse with cold water. Transfer pasta to a large bowl; add remaining ingredients and mix well. Cover and chill until serving time. Makes 6 to 8 servings.

Poppy Seed Garden Pasta Salad

Stephanie Carlson
Sioux Falls, SD

The poppy seed dressing is what makes this salad so special. It gives it a sweet little kick!

2 c. tri-color rotini pasta,
  uncooked
1 tomato, cut into bite-sized
  pieces
1 cucumber, quartered
  lengthwise and sliced

1/2 c. red onion, sliced
poppy seed salad dressing
  to taste

Cook pasta according to package directions; drain and rinse with cold water. Transfer pasta to a large bowl; chill for at least 30 minutes. Add vegetables and desired amount of salad dressing; mix well. Cover and chill until serving time. Makes 4 to 6 servings.

Sprinkle a tossed salad with ruby-red pomegranate seeds for a festive touch.

Back-to-School
FALL RECIPES

Saucy Golden Fruit Salad

Janis Parr
Ontario, Canada

*Everyone loves this rich, delicious fruit salad. It's perfect for
the buffet table and will be devoured before you know it.
You don't need to peel the apples...they'll add color to the salad.*

2 Red Delicious apples, cored
  and sliced
1 Golden Delicious apple, cored
  and sliced
2 c. seedless green grapes,
  halved

2 10-oz. cans mandarin oranges,
  drained
20-oz. can pineapple tidbits,
  drained
3 bananas, sliced

Combine all fruit in a large bowl and stir together. Pour hot Sauce over
fruit; stir to combine. Let stand, uncovered, until cool. Makes 6 to
8 servings.

Sauce:

2/3 c. orange juice
2 T. lemon juice

1 c. sugar
1/4 c. cornstarch

In a small pot, combine juices and sugar. Stir in cornstarch until
dissolved. Cook over medium heat, stirring constantly, until mixture
comes to a boil and thickens.

The bright colors of fresh fruit really shine in an antique cut-glass
bowl. When washing cut glass, add a little white vinegar to the
rinse water. The glass will sparkle...beautiful on a buffet table!

Kid-Friendly
VEGGIE DISHES

Ambrosia Salad

Ashley Simons
Lincoln Park, MI

*Is it a salad or a dessert? I work for a middle school and
we make this recipe to serve over eight hundred kids!*

10-oz. can mandarin oranges,
   drained
15-oz. can fruit cocktail, drained
1 c. sweetened flaked coconut

1 c. mini marshmallows
8-oz. container frozen whipped
   topping, thawed
1/2 c. sour cream

Combine all ingredients in a large bowl; mix well. Cover and chill before
serving. Makes 8 to 10 servings.

Waldorf Salad

Lori Simmons
Princeville, IL

*An old favorite that's a must at every family holiday dinner!
If you like, add raisins instead of nuts.*

4 to 5 apples, cored and diced
1 lb. seedless grapes, halved
2 bananas, sliced
1/2 c. chopped pecans or walnuts

3/4 c. frozen whipped topping,
   thawed
1/2 c. mayonnaise

In a large bowl, combine fruit and nuts. Fold in whipped topping and
mayonnaise; stir to coat well. Cover and chill for one hour. Makes
6 servings.

For packed lunches, freeze some juice boxes...by lunchtime,
they'll be thawed and ready to drink. They'll help keep
the rest of the lunch chilled too.

Back-to-School
FALL RECIPES

Trish's Cranberry Salad

Angel Fridley
Staunton, VA

This is a holiday favorite shared with us years ago by a special family friend. We especially love to enjoy it at Thanksgiving and Christmas!

14-oz. can whole-berry cranberry
    sauce
8-oz. can crushed pineapple
3-oz. pkg. cranberry gelatin mix
1 c. celery, diced

1 Granny Smith or Gala apple,
    peeled, cored and chopped
1/2 c. chopped pecans or walnuts
Garnish: whipped cream

In a saucepan, combine cranberry sauce, pineapple with juice and dry gelatin mix. Cook and stir over low heat for 10 to 15 minutes, until gelatin mix is completely dissolved, stirring occasionally to prevent scorching. Stir in celery, apple and nuts. Remove from heat; spoon mixture into a greased 6-cup gelatin mold. Cover and refrigerate for 8 hours or overnight. To serve, turn out of mold. Serve topped with whipped cream. Makes 8 servings.

Whenever you put away the groceries, label ingredients before refrigerating so they won't become snacks instead. Cheese cubes, fruit and veggies labeled "OK for snacking" are sure to tame appetites without upsetting your dinner plans.

Kid-Friendly
VEGGIE DISHES

Holiday Apple Salad

Sharon Tillman
Hampton, VA

Everyone loves the crunchy, sweet taste of this salad! It's terrific in fall and winter, since all the ingredients are available year 'round. A mix of apple and pear slices would be good too.

3 apples, cored and thinly sliced
juice of 1/2 lemon
12-oz. pkg. spring mix greens
1 c. chopped pecans or walnuts,
  toasted

3/4 c. sweetened dried
  cranberries
4-oz. pkg. crumbled blue cheese
apple cider vinaigrette salad
  dressing to taste

Place apple slices in a large plastic zipping bag. Drizzle with lemon juice; close bag and shake to coat. In a large salad bowl, layer salad greens, apple slices, nuts, cranberries and blue cheese. Just before serving, drizzle with salad dressing as desired. Toss until well coated and serve. Serves 8 to 10.

Fall always signaled the start of school for me. I am 70, and a retired kindergarten and first grade teacher. I've always loved school, ever since I started "pre-primary" in 1953! Loved school and all my grammar school teachers. Junior high and high school were fun too! In 1970, I went to college and became a teacher, and taught for 34 years. I loved my teaching career, and working with young children was always so rewarding. Shortly after I retired, I became a grandmother, and I was able to relive those September days of "back to school" with my grandsons. Fall will always bring happy schooltime memories for me!

– Rosemary Lightbown, Wakefield, RI

Back-to-School
FALL RECIPES

Spiced Apple-Stuffed Acorn Squash

Gail Blain
Grand Island, NE

It's no accident that winter squashes come along at just the same time as apples....they belong together! This recipe combines the two in an oh-so yummy way.

1 acorn squash, quartered and seeds removed	2 t. brown sugar, packed
1 Golden Delicious apple, peeled, cored and sliced	1/8 t. ground cloves
	1/8 t. cinnamon
	1/8 t. nutmeg
2 t. butter, melted	

Place squash pieces, cut-side down, in a greased 13"x9" baking pan. Cover and bake at 350 degrees for 30 minutes. Meanwhile, combine remaining ingredients in a bowl. Turn over squash, cut-side up; top with apple mixture. Cover and bake for 30 minutes longer, or until apples are tender. Serves 4.

Sweet Potato Fries

Tina Wright
Atlanta, GA

A tasty side for burgers and sandwiches! If you like them sweet, add 2 tablespoons brown sugar and 1/2 teaspoon cinnamon along with the oil and salt.

4 sweet potatoes, peeled and cut into strips	1 T. olive oil
	1 t. salt

Place sweet potato strips in a large bowl. Add oil and salt; toss well to coat. Arrange on a lightly greased baking sheet. Bake on center rack of oven at 425 degrees for 20 minutes. Turn over; bake another 15 minutes, or until tender. Serve immediately. Serves 4.

Keep apple pie spice on hand for fall cooking. A blend of cinnamon, nutmeg and allspice, it's like a whole spice rack in a little can.

Kid-Friendly
VEGGIE DISHES

Party Potatoes

Roberta Simpkins
Mentor on the Lake, OH

When we were kids, my mom always made these potatoes for parties and holidays. Everyone loved them! As kids, getting to crush the corn flakes to spread on top was the job we all wanted.

32-oz. pkg. frozen shredded
  hashbrowns
10-3/4 oz. can cream of potato
  soup
10-3/4 oz. can cream of celery
  soup

8-oz. container sour cream
1 onion, diced
8-oz. pkg. shredded sharp
  Cheddar cheese
1 c. corn flake cereal, crushed
1/4 c. butter, melted

In a lightly greased 13"x9" baking pan, combine hashbrowns, soups, sour cream, onion and cheese. Spread crushed cereal on top; drizzle with melted butter. Cover and bake at 325 degrees for one hour, or until bubbly and golden. Makes 8 servings.

Try mashed kabocha squash for a delicious change! Cut a kabocha squash in half. Scoop out the seeds and place squash halves cut-side down in a baking pan brushed with olive oil. Bake at 375 degrees until fork-tender, 45 to 60 minutes. Cool slightly. Scoop out the cooked squash and mash with butter, milk and maybe a touch of maple syrup. Yummy!

Back-to-School
FALL RECIPES

Cheesy Broccoli-Cauliflower

Cyn DeStefano
Hermitage, PA

This side dish is so easy to make! It is all done in the microwave and tastes so good, even the kids will ask for seconds. It's a great way to dress up veggies to go with any main dish.

1 lb. broccoli, cut into bite-size
    flowerets
1 lb. cauliflower, cut into
    bite-size flowerets
1/2 c. water
1/2 c. cream cheese

1/4 c. milk
1/2 c. sour cream
1-1/2 c. shredded Cheddar
    cheese
15 round buttery crackers
    crackers, crushed

Combine broccoli and cauliflower in a microwave-safe 2-quart casserole dish; add water. Cover and microwave on high for 10 minutes. Drain; set vegetables aside. In another microwafe-safe bowl, microwave cream cheese with milk for one minute. Stir until well blended and creamy; add sour cream and mix well. Spoon sour cream mixture over vegetables; sprinkle with shredded cheese. Microwave for 2 minutes, or until cheese is melted. Sprinkle with crushed crackers; microwave for one more minute. Serves 8.

A flexible plastic cutting mat makes speedy work of slicing & dicing. Keep 2 mats in different colors on hand for chopping meat and veggies separately.

Kid-Friendly
VEGGIE DISHES

Corn & Zucchini Toss

JoAnn
Gooseberry Patch

This is a tasty year 'round side dish that we all like. Add some diced tomato for color, if you wish.

4 slices bacon
2 c. zucchini, chopped
1-1/2 c. fresh or frozen corn
1/2 c. onion, chopped

1/8 t. pepper
1/4 c. shredded Monterey
  Jack cheese

In a large, deep skillet, cook bacon over medium-high heat until crisp. Drain bacon on paper towels, reserving drippings in pan. Add zucchini, corn and onion to reserved drippings; sauté over medium heat for about 10 minutes, until tender-crisp. Season with pepper. Transfer to a serving bowl; sprinkle with crumbled bacon and shredded cheese. Makes 5 servings.

Creamy Corn

Shannon Haga
Childress, TX

This recipe is very easy, takes just a few ingredients, and my husband loves it. He is a very picky eater!

16-oz. pkg. frozen corn
2 3-oz. pkgs. cream cheese,
  softened

3 T. butter, softened
salt and pepper to taste

In a saucepan, cook corn according to package directions; drain. Add remaining ingredients; stir until cream cheese and butter are melted. Makes 4 to 6 servings.

Whip up a tasty dip for sliced fruit. Simply swirl fruit preserves into plain Greek yogurt. Hungry kids will love it any time of day!

Back-to-School
FALL RECIPES

Cheesy Spinach Bake

Leona Krivda
Belle Vernon, PA

We all love spinach at my house, but if you can't get your kids to eat it, try this recipe. With all the cheese, they will love it!

10-oz. pkg. frozen chopped
  spinach, thawed and
  well drained
2 T. all-purpose flour
2 eggs, beaten
3-oz. pkg. cream cheese,
  softened and cubed

1 c. American cheese, cubed
1/4 c. butter, cubed
1-1/2 t. dried, minced onion
1/2 t. salt
1/2 c. dry bread crumbs
1/4 c. butter, melted
1/4 c. shredded Parmesan cheese

Place spinach in a lightly greased 1-1/2 quart casserole dish. Stir flour into spinach; fold in eggs, cream cheese, American cheese, cubed butter, onion and salt. Combine bread crumbs, melted butter and Parmesan cheese in a small bowl; sprinkle over top. Bake, uncovered, at 350 degrees for 30 minutes, or until heated through and cheese is melted. Serves 6.

Back-to-school time isn't just for kids. Treat yourself to
a class that you've been longing to try...whether it's knitting,
scrapbooking, yoga or even a foreign language. Take
a friend along for twice the fun!

Kid-Friendly
VEGGIE DISHES

Oven-Roasted Potatoes

Julia Grogan
Fleetwood, NC

*These potatoes are a family favorite. Every time I take this dish
somewhere, it disappears right away!*

5 redskin potatoes, cut into
   1-inch cubes
1/4 c. butter, diced
1/2 t. dried parsley

salt and pepper to taste
1/3 c. shredded Cheddar cheese
3 T. real bacon bits

In a large saucepan, cover potatoes with water. Bring to a boil over high
heat; simmer until potatoes are almost tender. Drain; spread potatoes in
a greased 13"x9" baking pan. Scatter butter around the potatoes;
sprinkle with parsley, salt, pepper and cheese. Top with bacon bits.
Bake, uncovered, at 400 degrees for 15 minutes, or until potatoes are
golden and cheese is bubbly. Makes 4 servings.

Take the whole family on a harvest scavenger hunt. Make a list
of fall finds...a red maple leaf, a pumpkin, an acorn, a scarecrow,
a red apple and a hay bale, just to name a few. It's not only
lots of fun, it's a great way to get outside and enjoy the
fabulous fall weather!

Back-to-School
FALL RECIPES

Carol's Crockery Beans

Carol Gray
Sammamish, WA

This slow-cooker recipe is a family favorite I got from my mom.
I am asked to bring it to potlucks year 'round! My husband and
son like to add some chopped jalapeño peppers on the side.

1 lb. ground beef
1/2 lb. bacon, chopped
1 c. onion, chopped
1 c. catsup
1 T. smoke-flavored
   cooking sauce

1 T. white vinegar
1 c. brown sugar, packed
21-oz. can red kidney beans,
   drained
21-oz. can baked beans, drained
21-oz. can pork & beans, drained

In a large skillet over medium heat, cook beef, bacon and onion until beef is browned and bacon is crisp. Drain and transfer to a 4-quart slow cooker. Stir in catsup, sauce, vinegar and brown sugar. Add beans and stir thoroughly. Cover and cook on high setting for 2 hours, or until hot and bubbly. Turn to low setting and cook for another 8 to 10 hours. Serves 10 to 12.

I love autumn, when the leaves change and swirl around. As children, how we loved romping in the leaves, running around the teepee cornstalks and anticipating the events of fall and winter. I remember coming home after school, with the crisp autumn air blowing woodsy aromas, and finding wonderful smells in the kitchen. Shorter days meant cozy evenings in the house. All those summer fruits and vegetables would become hearty meals for cold evenings. The colors of autumn and the changing of the season still take me back to carefree days.

– Sharon Thornhill, Pottstown, PA

Kid-Friendly
VEGGIE DISHES

Pioneer Scalloped Corn Casserole *Tracie Carlson*
Richardson, TX

This dish disappears fast! When our son was young and a picky eater, we added "Pioneer" to the name of this recipe because he liked Western history. It quickly became a top favorite of his. I often double this, using a 13"x9" pan and baking for about 70 minutes. It's yummy garnished with crispy chopped bacon.

2 eggs, beaten
12-oz. can evaporated milk
3/4 c. onion, chopped
1/3 c. sugar
1 t. garlic salt

1 t. pepper
2 15-oz. cans creamed corn
47 saltine crackers, crushed
1/4 c. butter, diced
salt and pepper to taste

In a large bowl, combine eggs, milk, onion, sugar and seasonings; mix well. Fold in corn; mix in crushed crackers until thoroughly combined. Transfer mixture to a buttered deep 9"x9" baking pan. Dot with butter; season with additional salt and pepper. Bake, uncovered, at 350 degrees for 45 minutes to one hour, until set and golden around the edges. Makes 6 servings.

Have little ones make a cookbook of their favorite foods. It's OK if "Mackerony and Chezze" bakes for 300 hours and "Chican Nuggtts" are made with "2 chickans and a big jar of soss." Make sure they put their names on their recipes! Staple recipes into a booklet...sure to bring back sweet memories years from now.

Back-to-School
FALL RECIPES

Granny's Sweet Potato Casserole
Julie Marsh
Shelbyville, TN

It didn't have to be a holiday for Granny Hodge to make this casserole. She always made another small dish with extra marshmallows, just for us kids.

2-1/2 lbs. sweet potatoes, peeled and cubed
3/4 c. brown sugar, packed
1/4 c. butter, softened
1-1/2 t. salt

1/2 t. vanilla extract
1/2 c. pecans, finely chopped and divided
2 c. mini marshmallows

In a Dutch oven, cover sweet potatoes with cold water. Bring to a boil over high heat; reduce heat to medium. Simmer for 15 minutes, or until very tender. Drain; transfer potatoes to a large bowl and cool slightly. Add brown sugar, butter, salt and vanilla; mash mixture with a potato masher. Fold in 1/4 cup pecans. Spread evenly in an 11"x7" baking pan coated with non-stick vegetable spray. Sprinkle with remaining pecans; top with marshmallows. Bake, uncovered, at 375 degrees for 25 minutes, or until golden. Serves 6.

Let everyone in the family help make dinner! Younger children can tear lettuce for salad...older kids can measure and chop ingredients or stir a skillet.

Carly's Green Bean Casserole

Carly St. Clair
Amarillo, TX

I remember how my grandma made green bean casserole at Thanksgiving and Christmas...these are very fond memories for me. My husband doesn't care for mushrooms or mushroom soup, so I've come up with my own version of this favorite. Everyone loves it.

1 lb. fresh green beans, trimmed
  and cut into bite-size pieces
10-3/4 oz. can cream of
  celery soup

1/2 c. plus 2 T. milk
1 c. slivered almonds,
  divided

Place beans in a buttered 1-1/2 quart casserole dish. Add soup, milk and 1/2 cup almonds; stir thoroughly. Top with remaining almonds. Bake, uncovered, at 375 degrees for 30 minutes, or until hot and bubbly. Makes 6 to 8 servings.

Butter & Honey Glazed Carrots

Dianne Young
Salt Lake City, UT

A wonderful side dish for any family gathering or dinner party.

2 lbs. baby carrots
1/4 c. brown sugar, packed

1/4 c. honey
1/4 c. butter

In a saucepan, cover carrots with water; bring to a boil over high heat. Reduce heat to medium; simmer until tender and drain. In a small saucepan, combine remaining ingredients; cook and stir over low heat until brown sugar dissolves. Drizzle over cooked carrots and stir. Makes 6 to 8 servings.

to: Grandma
xoxo

A quick fall craft for kids...hot glue large acorn caps onto round magnets for whimsical fridge magnets.

81

Back-to-School
FALL RECIPES

Creamy Vegetable Medley

Dianne Cook
New Milford, CT

My son requests this dish every Thanksgiving and Christmas.
I'm often asked to bring it to potlucks at church too.

16-oz. pkg. frozen broccoli,
  cauliflower & carrot
  combination, thawed
  and drained
10-3/4 oz. can reduced-fat cream
  of mushroom soup
1/3 c. sour cream

1/4 t. pepper
1 c. shredded Gruyère or Swiss
  cheese, divided
2.8-oz. can French fried onions,
  divided
Optional: 4-oz. jar chopped
  pimentos, drained

In a bowl, combine vegetables, soup, sour cream, pepper, 1/2 cup
cheese, 1/2 can onions and pimento, if using. Spoon into a lightly
greased one-quart casserole dish. Cover and bake at 350 degrees for
30 minutes. Uncover; top with remaining cheese and onions. Bake,
uncovered, for 5 minutes longer, or until bubbly and cheese is melted.
Serves 6.

A cherished family recipe can be a super conversation starter.
Take time to share family stories and traditions with
your kids over the dinner table!

Kid-Friendly VEGGIE DISHES

Creamy Mashed Potatoes

Mel Chencharick
Julian, PA

Made with chicken broth instead of water, these potatoes are so good! Sweet potatoes can also be used in this recipe. Serve with butter or your best gravy.

2-1/2 lbs. potatoes, peeled and cut into 1-inch cubes
3-1/2 c. chicken broth

1/2 c. light cream
2 T. butter
pepper to taste

In a large saucepan, combine potatoes and broth. Bring to a boil over high heat; reduce heat to medium. Cover and cook 10 minutes, or until potatoes are fork-tender. Drain potatoes well in a colander, reserving broth; transfer potatoes to a bowl. Mash potatoes with 1/4 cup reserved broth, cream and butter; season generously with pepper. Add reserved broth, if needed, to desired consistency. Makes 5 servings.

No-Fry French Fries

Gladys Kielar
Whitehouse, OH

This is the only kind of French fries we make now...try them and you'll prefer them too!

2 baking potatoes
1/4 c. grated Parmesan cheese
1/2 t. paprika

1/8 t. pepper
salt to taste

Cut potatoes lengthwise into thin wedges; spray with non-stick vegetable spray and place in a plastic zipping bag. Combine cheese, paprika and pepper; add to bag and shake to coat well. Arrange potatoes in a single layer on a lightly sprayed 15"x10" jelly-roll pan. Bake at 425 degrees for 30 minutes, or until crisp and tender, turning once. Season with salt. Serves 4.

A yummy sauce for French fries! Combine 1/4 cup mayo, 2 big spoonfuls of catsup and a teaspoon of vinegar.

Back-to-School
FALL RECIPES

Tomato-Squash Sauté

Mary Dierschow
State Center, IA

*This is a favorite creation of my mother's. Another yummy way
to use those zucchini...we love it!*

1 T. butter
1 zucchini, sliced
1 yellow squash, sliced
3/4 c. onion, sliced

3 roma tomatoes, quartered
1 T. salt-free seasoning
1/3 c. shredded Swiss cheese

Melt butter in a skillet over medium-low heat. Add vegetables; sprinkle
with seasoning. Cover and cook for about 20 minutes, stirring
occasionally. Uncover and sprinkle cheese over vegetables. Reduce
heat to low; cover and cook for 3 minutes, or until cheese melts.
Serves 2 to 3.

Toasted pumpkin seeds are a delicious fall treat! Rinse 2 cups of
seeds well; drain on paper towels and pat dry. Toss the seeds with
one tablespoon of olive oil and spread on an ungreased baking
sheet. Bake at 350 degrees for 20 minutes; or until golden,
stirring every 5 minutes. Sprinkle with salt and cool.

Kid-Friendly
VEGGIE DISHES

Quick & Easy Rice Pilaf

Sharon Laney
Maryville, TN

A friend from church brought this to a potluck dinner over 30 years ago and it's become a favorite side. Chopped broccoli and/or mushrooms may be added. You can even add some cooked, diced chicken to make it a main dish.

1 c. celery, chopped
1 c. onion, chopped
6 T. butter

1 c. white or brown long-cooking
rice, uncooked
2 c. chicken or beef broth

In a skillet over medium heat, sauté celery and onion in butter for 5 minutes. Add uncooked rice; cook for one to 2 minutes. Add broth. Cover and cook for 15 to 20 minutes, until broth is absorbed and rice is tender. Serves 6.

Cabbage & Noodles

Kelly Alderson
Erie, PA

This old-fashioned dish is delicious with grilled sausage.

8-oz. pkg. wide egg noodles,
uncooked
1 cabbage, chopped
3/4 c. butter, divided

1 t. salt
pepper to taste
1 T. poppy seed

Cook noodles according to package directions; drain. Meanwhile, bring a saucepan of water to a boil over high heat. Add cabbage and cook for 5 minutes; drain. Melt 1/2 cup butter in same saucepan. Sauté cabbage over low heat for 15 minutes, stirring often; season with salt and pepper. Combine hot noodles with remaining butter and poppy seed. Transfer cabbage to a serving dish; top with noodles. Serves 6.

If you were to ask me what is most important in a home,
I would say memories.
– Lillian Gish

Back-to-School
FALL RECIPES

Pumpkin Pie Applesauce

Andrea Heyart
Savannah, TX

This wonderfully unique applesauce is just as delicious warm as it is chilled. Adjust the amount of sugar according to how naturally sweet your apples are and to suit your taste.

6 apples, peeled, cored
   and diced
2/3 c. apple cider or juice
2/3 c. canned pumpkin

1/4 c. brown sugar, packed,
   or to taste
2 t. pumpkin pie spice
1/4 t. cinnamon

Combine all ingredients in a large saucepan; bring to a low boil over medium heat. Reduce heat to medium-low and simmer for about 30 minutes, until apples are very soft and tender. Using a potato masher, an electric mixer or an immersion blender, purée applesauce mixture to desired consistency. Serve warm or chilled. Makes 10 servings.

Apple picking can be a fun family outing! The kids will be amazed to see all the different kinds of apples and so many are just the right size for little ones. Take a picnic and make a day of it, with fresh-picked apples for dessert!

FAMILY FAVORITES
for Dinnertime

Spaghetti Hot Dish

Debbie Erling
Sparks, NV

This is fast and easy. My children loved it when they were little. Even now, it's my husband's favorite and my grandchildren's favorite too. I have frozen half and reheated it on a rainy day. It's even better the second time around!

8-oz. pkg. spaghetti, uncooked
   and broken in half
2 lbs. ground beef
2 10-3/4 oz. cans tomato soup
10-3/4 oz. can cream of
   mushroom soup

2 c. milk
1/4 c. dried, minced onion
salt and pepper to taste
1-1/2 c. shredded Cheddar
   cheese, divided

Cook spaghetti according to package directions; drain. Meanwhile, brown beef in a skillet over medium heat; drain. Transfer spaghetti to a greased 13"x9" baking pan. Add beef and remaining ingredients, reserving 1/2 cup cheese for topping; mix gently. Bake, uncovered, at 350 degrees for 45 minutes to one hour, until hot and golden on top. Sprinkle with reserved cheese; return to oven for several minutes, until cheese has melted. Let stand 5 minutes before serving. Makes 6 to 8 servings.

Set a regular dinner theme for each night and it'll be a snap to make out your shopping list. Some tasty, kid-friendly themes are Taco Night, Spaghetti Night and Chili Night... your family is sure to think of other favorites too!

FAMILY FAVORITES
for Dinnertime

Pierogies & Meatballs Casserole

Melissa Flasck
Rochester Hills, MI

My little son loves eating mini meatballs, so I wanted to create a recipe to get him to try some new foods with one of his favorites. It's fast and easy to put together...we can play while we wait for it to cook! Serve with a tossed salad and garlic bread.

32-oz. jar favorite spaghetti
  sauce, divided
16-oz. pkg. frozen potato and
  cheese pierogies, uncooked

16-oz. pkg. frozen bite-size
  meatballs
8-oz. pkg. shredded mozzarella
  cheese

Spread half of spaghetti sauce in the bottom of a greased 13"x9" baking pan. Arrange pierogies over sauce; layer meatballs in between. Spread cheese over top. Cover with aluminum foil. Bake at 350 degrees for 35 to 40 minutes, until heated through. Serves 6.

Italian Chicken & Rice

Diane Cohen
Breinigsville, PA

This is so convenient! I usually have all the ingredients on hand. In the morning, it's easy to put together in the slow cooker, then I only have to fix rice and steam broccoli for a delicious dinner!

10-3/4 oz. can cream of chicken
  soup
8-oz. pkg. cream cheese,
  softened
0.7-oz. pkg. Italian salad
  dressing mix

4 boneless, skinless chicken
  breasts
cooked rice

In a 4-quart slow cooker, stir together soup, cream cheese and Italian dressing mix. Place chicken breasts in slow cooker; spoon soup mixture over chicken. Cover and cook on low setting for 7 to 8 hours, or on high setting for 4 hours, until chicken is very tender. Using 2 forks, shred chicken in the slow cooker; stir into soup mixture. To serve, spoon over hot cooked rice. Serves 5 to 6.

Back-to-School
FALL RECIPES

Caribbean Chicken

Courtney Stultz
Weir, KS

This is a very simple recipe using easy-to-find ingredients.
It's a great quick-fix meal for busy nights during the week.
Serve with steamed vegetables for a complete meal.

4 boneless, skinless chicken
    breasts, cut into chunks
2 T. olive oil
2 to 3 t. garlic salt
14-1/2 oz. can fire-roasted
    diced tomatoes, drained

20-oz. can pineapple chunks,
    drained
1/4 c. barbecue sauce
cooked rice

In a large skillet, combine chicken chunks, oil and garlic salt; toss to coat. Cook over medium heat for about 15 minutes, or until chicken is cooked through, tossing occasionally. Add tomatoes, pineapple and barbecue sauce; toss well to combine. Cook an additional 5 minutes, or until heated through. Serve over cooked rice. Serves 4.

After my sister Jane graduated from high school, she moved to the "city" to work. There, she made many new friends who had rarely been to the country, and definitely not to a small farm like ours. They enjoyed coming "down home" with her on weekends to help with harvest and whatever chores they could chip in with. My mother would fret, because our farmhouse was much less than what they were used to. She would prepare bountiful meals, and we had great times together, even while working hard.

                    –Judy Taylor, Butler, MO

FAMILY FAVORITES
for Dinnertime

Super-Easy Chicken & Stuffing Bake

Maureen Wiwad
Alberta, Canada

This casserole is fun to make and very filling. The grandkids love it! I serve this dish with mashed potatoes and a salad. If your family likes more stuffing, you can use 2 boxes to really cover the dish. It can be prepared ahead of time and kept in the fridge, as it does not take long to bake.

1 c. water
6-oz. pkg. chicken-flavored
  stuffing mix
2 to 3 boneless, skinless chicken
  breasts, cubed

10-3/4 oz. can cream of chicken,
  celery or mushroom soup
1/3 c. sour cream
3 c. frozen mixed vegetables,
  thawed and drained

In a saucepan over high heat, bring water to a boil. Add stuffing mix; stir until moistened and set aside. In a greased 13"x9" baking pan, mix together remaining ingredients. Sprinkle stuffing over top. Bake, uncovered, at 400 degrees for 30 to 40 minutes, until heated through and chicken is cooked. Makes 3 to 4 servings.

Handprint turkeys are a Thanksgiving classic! Turn the kids loose, drawing turkeys around their hands on a stack of folded large index cards. Add the names of family & friends joining you for the big day...they'll be charmed.

Back-to-School
FALL RECIPES

Mom's Beef Stroganoff

Denise Webb
Newington, GA

I used to love walking into the house after school on a cold winter's day and smell this stroganoff cooking on the stove. And 50 years later, it's still one of my favorites...it is so comforting and delicious!

1-1/2 lb. ground beef
1.35-oz. pkg. onion soup mix
3 T. all-purpose flour
2 T. tomato paste

8-oz. pkg. sliced mushrooms
2-1/2 c. water
1/2 c. sour cream
cooked egg noodles

Brown beef in a large skillet over medium heat; drain. Blend in soup mix, flour, tomato paste and mushrooms. Stir in water; cover and simmer for 10 minutes. Stir in sour cream just before serving; Serve over cooked noodles. Makes 4 to 6 servings.

Celebrate Grandparents' Day, September 12, by inviting Grandma & Grandpa to dinner. Let them take it easy while the rest of the family does all the cooking and serving! It's a great time for the kids to tell everyone about their new school year.

FAMILY FAVORITES
for Dinnertime

Poor Man's Beef Stew

Jacquelyn Tobin
Mahanoy City, PA

*This is something my grandmother used to make for me when
I went to her house for lunch during school. Enjoy with
some nice crusty rolls and butter.*

1 lb. lean ground beef
2-1/2 lbs. potatoes, peeled
  and sliced
2 to 3 carrots, peeled and cut
  into chunks

2 stalks celery, cut into chunks
1 c. onion, halved and sliced
10-3/4 oz. can tomato soup
1-1/4 c. water
1 t. white vinegar

Brown beef in a skillet over medium heat; drain. In a lightly greased
13"x9" baking pan, layer half each of beef, potatoes, carrots, celery and
onion. Repeat layering. In a bowl, whisk together soup, water and
vinegar. Pour soup mixture over all; cover with aluminum foil. Bake at
350 degrees for 90 minutes, or until hot and bubbly. Makes 6 servings.

As autumn evenings turn dark, light a candle or 2 at the family
dinner table. It'll make an ordinary meal seem special!

Favorite Baked Penne

Alicia Null
Mechanicsburg, PA

*I have four young daughters who are very picky eaters,
but this is one dish that they all gobble down!*

16-oz. pkg. mezze penne pasta,
  uncooked
2 eggs, beaten
15-oz. container ricotta cheese
2/3 c. grated Parmesan cheese
2 t. Italian seasoning

1/2 t. salt
1/4 t. pepper
16-oz. pkg. shredded mozzarella
  cheese, divided
45-oz. jar spaghetti sauce,
  divided

Cook pasta according to package directions; drain. Meanwhile, in a
very large bowl, mix eggs, ricotta cheese, Parmesan cheese, seasonings,
3 cups mozzarella cheese and 3/4 jar spaghetti sauce. Add pasta; mix
together and transfer to a greased 13"x9" baking pan. Top with
remaining spaghetti sauce and mozzarella cheese. Bake, uncovered,
at 350 degrees for 30 minutes, or until bubbly and cheese is melted.
Makes 10 servings.

The number-one tip for speedy weeknight meals! Before you
start cooking, read the recipe all the way through and
make sure you have everything you'll need. No more
quick runs to the store!

FAMILY FAVORITES
for Dinnertime

Steve's Macaroni & Cheese

Karen McCann
Marion, OH

My son made this in home economics class back in 1989 and he said it was the best he'd ever tasted. So he made it for our family and it has been a favorite ever since. I hope you love it as much as we do!

1 c. elbow macaroni, uncooked
2 T. butter
3 T. all-purpose flour
1/2 t. salt
1/8 t. pepper

1 c. milk
3/4 c. pasteurized process
  cheese, diced
Optional: 1/2 c. buttery cracker
  crumbs, 1 T. butter, melted

Cook macaroni according to package directions; drain. Transfer macaroni to a buttered 8"x8" baking pan; set aside. Meanwhile, melt butter in a saucepan over medium heat. Remove from heat; add flour and seasonings. Stir until all lumps have been dissolved. Slowly add milk to flour mixture and return to heat, stirring until sauce thickens. Add cheese; stir until melted and well blended. Pour cheese sauce over macaroni. If desired, mix cracker crumbs and melted butter; sprinkle over top. Bake, uncovered, at 350 degrees for 20 to 30 minutes, until bubbly and heated through. Makes 4 to 6 servings.

I have found the best way to give advice to your children is to find out what they want, and then advise them to do it.
– Harry S. Truman

Back-to-School
FALL RECIPES

Corn Chip Chicken

Lynn Long
Greensboro, NC

I found this recipe over 20 years ago on the back of a shredded cheese package. It has been served for many children's birthdays and weekly meals. It is always the dinner requested when the kids have a friend over for dinner. I always double the recipe...the next morning, everyone wants the leftovers for breakfast!

4 boneless, skinless chicken
   breasts, flattened to 1/2-inch
   thick
10-3/4 oz. can cream of chicken
   soup
3/4 c. milk

1-oz. pkg. taco seasoning mix
8-oz. pkg. shredded sharp
   Cheddar cheese
6-oz. pkg. corn chips
cooked brown rice

Arrange chicken in a 13"x9" baking pan coated with non-stick vegetable spray. In a bowl, combine soup, milk, taco seasoning and cheese; spoon over chicken. Top chicken with corn chips; cover with aluminum foil. Bake at 350 degrees for 50 minutes, or until chicken juices run clear when pierced. Serve with cooked rice. Makes 4 servings.

Chile Relleno Casserole

Lori Frey
Satanta, KS

A very easy meatless dish! Everyone's favorite at our house.

2 7-oz. cans whole green chile
   peppers, drained
8-oz. pkg. shredded Monterey
   Jack cheese, divided
8-oz. pkg. shredded Cheddar
   cheese, divided

5-oz. can evaporated milk
1/2 c. milk
2 eggs, beaten
2 T. all-purpose flour
1/2 to 2/3 c. tomato sauce

In a greased 13"x9" baking pan, layer one can chiles and half of each cheese. Repeat layering. In a bowl, whisk together milks, eggs and flour; pour over top. Cover and bake at 350 degrees for 25 minutes. Uncover; spoon tomato sauce over top. Bake, uncovered, 15 minutes longer. Serves 6.

FAMILY FAVORITES
for Dinnertime

Teresa's Oven-Fried Chicken Tenders

Teresa Eller
Kansas City, KS

This is a great recipe when it's cold outside and you want to use the oven. Leftovers make great chicken sandwiches.

1/2 c. mayonnaise
1 T. chili powder
1/3 c. Italian-seasoned dry
   bread crumbs

1/3 c. grated Parmesan cheese
12 boneless, skinless chicken
   tenders

Line a baking sheet with aluminum foil; spray with non-stick vegetable spray and set aside. Mix mayonnaise and chili powder in a shallow dish; set aside. Mix bread crumbs and cheese in another dish. Roll chicken tenders in mayonnaise mixture, then in crumb mixture; arrange on baking sheet. Bake at 350 degrees for 20 minutes; turn over and bake another 20 minutes. Serves 6.

At-the-Ranch Chicken Tenders

Kathie High
Lititz, PA

This chicken is great as a main dish. For a lighter meal, I also like to slice the chicken and serve it on top of a tossed salad.

1/2 c. fat-free ranch salad
   dressing
1 c. wheat & rice flake cereal,
   crushed

2 t. Italian seasoning or chili
   powder
1 lb. boneless, skinless chicken
   tenders

Place salad dressing in a shallow dish; mix cereal crumbs and seasoning in another dish. Coat chicken tenders with dressing; coat well in crumb mixture. Arrange on an aluminum foil-covered baking sheet. Bake at 425 degrees for 20 minutes, or until juices run clear when pierced. Makes 4 servings.

An easy dipping sauce for chicken tenders! Mix up 1/3 cup catsup, 2 tablespoons maple syrup, 1/2 teaspoon soy sauce and 1/2 teaspoon Worcestershire sauce.

Back-to-School
FALL RECIPES

Creamy Tortellini & Sausage Skillet Supper

Wendy D'Angelo
Brookhaven, PA

This recipe was shared with me by a dear friend and quickly became a family favorite. It is so quick & easy to prepare, it's no wonder that we enjoy it often! It looks special, but is simple enough to toss together on any busy weeknight. Serve with warm, crusty bread.

10-oz. pkg. frozen cheese
   tortellini, uncooked
1 lb. smoked pork sausage, sliced
1/2 c. white onion, diced
2 to 3 t. oil
14-1/2 oz. can petite diced
   tomatoes with onion and
   garlic

3-oz. pkg. cream cheese,
   softened
6-oz. pkg. fresh baby spinach

Cook tortellini according to package directions; drain. Meanwhile, in a large skillet over medium heat, cook sausage and onion in oil until sausage is lightly golden and onion is softened. Add tomatoes with juice; heat through. Add cream cheese; stir gently until melted and creamy. Add spinach; cover pan and let stand several minutes to allow spinach to steam slightly. Uncover and mix spinach into sauce; it will wilt down. Fold in tortellini and serve. Serves 4.

Make grilled bread to go with dinner. Slice a loaf of French bread nearly through. Spread slices with a mixture of 3/4 cup shredded cheese, 1/2 cup butter, 1/4 cup chopped fresh parsley, 1 teaspoon paprika and 3 to 4 cloves of minced garlic. Wrap up in aluminum foil and cook on a closed grill for about 15 minutes, turning once. Tasty!

FAMILY FAVORITES
for Dinnertime

Pork & Sauerkraut with Apples

Tyson Ann Trecannelli
Falling Waters, WV

Even the kids and picky eaters who aren't fond of sauerkraut will love this one! Apples are the surprise ingredient that really mellows the flavor in this slow-cooker recipe. Serve with mashed potatoes for a complete comfort food meal. Everyone comes back for more!

32-oz. pkg. refrigerated sauerkraut, drained and very well rinsed
2 apples, peeled, cored and cubed

4 country-style bone-in pork ribs
1-1/3 c. apple cider
mashed potatoes

Place sauerkraut in a 5-quart slow cooker set on high; mix in apples. Place ribs on top; pour cider over all. Reduce to low setting; cover and cook for 8 hours, or until ribs are tender. Remove ribs to a plate. Shred pork and mix into sauerkraut, discarding bones. Cover and continue cooking on low setting another 30 to 40 minutes. Serve pork and sauerkraut with mashed potatoes. Makes 6 servings.

When the kids are studying another country in school, why not try out a food from that country? Let them help choose a recipe and shop for the ingredients...you'll all learn so much together and have fun doing it!

Back-to-School
FALL RECIPES

Herbed Turkey Breast

Amy Butcher
Columbus, GA

*Brining is the secret trick that makes this turkey juicy and delicious!
It isn't hard at all, just a bit of prep ahead of time. Everyone at
the Thanksgiving dinner table will love it.*

9 c. water
3/4 c. salt
1/2 c. sugar
4 to 6-lb. bone-in whole turkey
   breast, thawed if frozen
1 onion, cut into 8 wedges

2 fresh rosemary sprigs
4 fresh thyme sprigs
3 bay leaves
6 T. butter, melted
1/4 c. chicken broth

In a 6-quart stockpot, combine water, salt and sugar; stir until sugar
and salt are dissolved. Add turkey breast. Cover and refrigerate for
12 to 24 hours. Remove turkey, discarding brine; rinse thoroughly
under cool running water and pat dry. Arrange onion and herbs on a
rack in a large roasting pan. Place turkey on rack, skin-side up. In a
bowl, combine butter and broth. Bake, uncovered, at 325 degrees for
1-1/2 hours; baste with butter mixture after one hour, and again after
30 minutes. Turn turkey skin-side down in pan. Bake another 30 to
60 minutes, continuing to baste, until a meat thermometer inserted in
thickest part reads 165 degrees. Remove to a platter; let stand
15 minutes before carving. Serves 8.

Keep little ones busy and happy with a crafting area
while the grown-ups put the finishing touches on Thanksgiving
dinner. Set out paper plates to decorate with colored paper,
feathers, pom-poms, crayons and washable glue. They'll be
proud to share their creations!

FAMILY FAVORITES
for Dinnertime

Country Filling Bake

James Bohner
Harrisburg, PA

*This homestyle dressing is a huge hit with all my family & friends.
I make it for every holiday and for all our church events. My wife
insists I make a double batch and tuck one in the freezer, for a quick
side during the week. It's also great for stuffed chicken breasts.*

16 c. bread cubes
2 eggs, beaten
2 c. milk
2 c. onions, chopped
1/2 c. celery, chopped

1/2 c. butter
2 T. dried parsley
1 T. salt
1 t. pepper
Optional: 1 T. dried sage

The night before, place bread cubes in a large bowl to dry out slightly,
stirring occasionally. Add eggs and milk; stir until well moistened and
set aside. In a skillet over medium heat, cook onions and celery in butter
until golden. Spoon onion mixture over bread cubes; add seasonings
and mix well. Transfer to a greased 3-quart casserole dish. Bake,
uncovered, at 350 degrees for one hour, or until heated through. Makes
8 to 10 servings.

When I was growing up, our Thanksgiving dinners (and many
other family dinners as well) were celebrated at our grandparents'
home. It was so amazing to walk into the house and smell all the
wonderful food that "Mom Mom" had prepared. Now I am a
grandmother myself and I host our family Thanksgiving dinner.
A few years ago, my brother walked into the kitchen and said,
"It smells just like Mom Mom's!" I'll never forget that.
I felt so blessed!
– Rebecca Glotfelty, LaVale, MD

Back-to-School
FALL RECIPES

Mom's Mexican Rice

Trysha Mapley-Barron
Wasilla, AK

I grew up on this wonderful stuff! Mom was a busy, busy lady between work, Girl Scouts, volunteering, friends...and taking care of the three of us to boot. With a salad on the side, this is an easy one-dish weeknight meal. So simple, so homey and delicious!

1 lb. lean ground beef
1 c. onion, chopped
1 c. green pepper, chopped
3 cloves garlic, minced
1 c. long-grain rice, uncooked
1/3 c. extra-virgin olive oil
3-1/2 c. tomato juice

1 T. chili powder
1/2 t. ground cumin
1/2 t. dried Mexican oregano
1 t. salt
pepper to taste
4-oz. can sliced mushrooms,
    drained

In a skillet over medium heat, cook beef with onion, pepper and garlic until beef is browned and onion and garlic are soft and fragrant. Add rice, oil, tomato juice and seasonings; mix together well. Stir in mushrooms and bring to a boil. Reduce heat to medium-low. Cover and simmer for 20 to 30 minutes, until liquid is absorbed and rice is cooked through. Serves 6.

Make it meatless: Delicious on its own, or stuffed into warm tortillas and topped with cheese and hot sauce. Follow recipe as given, but omit beef and cook vegetables in one tablespoon oil. During the last 5 minutes of cooking, stir in a drained 16-ounce can of pinto beans; heat through.

Younger guests will feel so grown up when served bubbly sparkling cider in long-stemmed plastic glasses. Decorate with curling ribbons just for fun.

FAMILY FAVORITES
for Dinnertime

Texas Spaghetti

Judy Henfey
Cibolo, TX

When I first moved to Texas, a neighbor made this dish for a potluck and it quickly became a family favorite. It's good to take to a new neighbor or a young family who may need a break from the kitchen. I always attach a copy of the recipe if I am delivering it to someone. Don't be afraid to experiment with the cheese...and season to taste.

16-oz. pkg. spaghetti, uncooked
1 lb. ground beef
3/4 c. onion, chopped
3/4 c. green pepper, chopped
2 10-3/4 oz. cans tomato soup
15-oz. can corn, plain or with
   diced peppers, drained

8-oz. pkg. pasteurized process
   cheese, chopped
Optional: 4-oz. can sliced black
   olives, drained

Cook spaghetti according to package directions; drain. Meanwhile, in a skillet over medium heat, cook beef, onion and pepper until beef is browned; drain. Stir in soup, corn, cheese and olives, if using. Add cooked spaghetti; toss well. Transfer to a lightly greased 13"x9" baking pan. Bake, uncovered, at 350 degrees for 30 minutes, until bubbly and cheese melts. Makes 8 servings.

Cloth napkins make mealtime just a little more special...
and they're a must when spaghetti is on the menu! Glue
colorful wooden letters from a craft store to napkin rings,
so family members can identify their own napkin easily.

Back-to-School
FALL RECIPES

Butter-Roasted Turkey Drumsticks

Cheri Maxwell
Gulf Breeze, FL

My boys think this is such a treat...and it's so much cheaper at home than at the county fair!

4 turkey drumsticks
1/2 c. butter, softened

salt and pepper to taste

Pat drumsticks dry with paper towels. With your hands, rub butter all over drumsticks and under the skin, if possible. Sprinkle generously with salt and pepper. Place drumsticks on a wire rack in a roasting pan. Bake, uncovered, at 350 degrees for 45 minutes. Turn drumsticks over. Bake an additional 45 minutes, or until juices run clear when pierced and a meat thermometer inserted in the thickest part reads 165 degrees. Let stand 10 minutes before serving. Makes 4 servings.

Chicken in a Pot

Shirley Howie
Foxboro, MA

This is a super-easy way to slow-cook a whole chicken. It creates very tender, juicy chicken! Great sliced and served on its own... perfect for all those recipes that call for cooked chicken too.

2 t. poultry seasoning
1 t. paprika
1/2 t. garlic powder

1 t. salt
4 to 5-lb. whole chicken

Combine seasonings in a small bowl; rub all over the chicken. Place chicken in a 6-quart slow cooker. Cover and cook on high setting for 2-1/2 to 3 hours, until a meat thermometer reads 165 degrees and juices run clear. Let stand for 10 minutes before slicing. Makes 4 to 6 servings.

FAMILY FAVORITES
for Dinnertime

Best Grilled Chicken

Hollie Moots
Marysville, OH

Each year, a local church congregation cooks a wonderful lunch for the staff at the school where I work. We always rave about it! They were kind enough to share the recipe with us. My family enjoys it all summer long and even into the warm days of fall.

10 boneless, skinless chicken breasts or other pieces	5 T. catsup
1 c. cider vinegar	1 T. Worcestershire sauce
1/2 c. oil	1/2 t. poultry seasoning
1 egg	2 T. salt
	1/4 t. pepper

Place chicken pieces in a large plastic zipping bag or covered plastic container. Combine remaining ingredients in a blender; process until well mixed and pour over chicken. Refrigerate up to 3 days, turning pieces occasionally; the longer it marinates, the richer the flavor. Drain, discarding marinade. Arrange chicken on a hot grill over medium heat. Grill about 5 to 7 minutes per side, depending on size of pieces, until golden and chicken juices run clear when pierced. Makes 10 servings.

One day when I was a junior in high school, I was walking the halls before class. I saw another student sitting by herself. I walked up and introduced myself, and we planned to meet for lunch. We became friends, and since 1963, she has been one of my best friends. The story ends there, but it is not the beginning. You see, one year earlier, I was that girl. It took two weeks before someone approached me and took me around like that. You never know when an act of kindness can turn into a lifelong friendship.

– Diane Himpelmann, Ringwood, IL

Back-to-School
FALL RECIPES

Our Family Favorite Casserole
Trudy Satterwhite
San Antonio, TX

This beef and noodle dish is our family's favorite casserole and a very good company dish. We have decided that it's a must-have for our family get-togethers.

2 c. medium egg noodles, uncooked
1 T. olive oil
1 lb. ground beef
8-oz. can tomato sauce
8-oz. pkg. cream cheese, softened

1 c. small-curd cottage cheese
1/2 c. light sour cream
1/3 c. green onions, minced
1-1/2 t. dried oregano
1/4 t. dried basil
salt and pepper to taste

Cook noodles according to package directions; drain. Meanwhile, heat oil in a large skillet over medium heat; add beef. Sauté until browned; drain. Stir in tomato sauce; remove from heat. In a large bowl, combine remaining ingredients. Spread half of noodles in a greased 13"x9" baking pan; cover with cheese mixture. Top with remaining noodles; spoon beef mixture over noodles. Bake, uncovered, at 375 degrees for 45 minutes, or until hot and bubbly. Makes 6 to 8 servings.

Start family meals with a gratitude circle...each person takes a moment to share something that he or she is thankful for that day. It's a sure way to put everyone in a cheerful mood!

FAMILY FAVORITES
for Dinnertime

Hamburger & Potato Casserole
Lisa Ivie
Paragould, AR

This casserole is perfect to make the night before and pop in the oven the next day. Great for cold nights, but if your family is like mine, it's delicious anytime. My mom made this for our family and now I make it for my own family. It's simple, easy and a must-try. Serve with a side of green beans or sweet corn.

2 lbs. ground beef
salt and pepper to taste
6 to 8 redskin potatoes,
    thinly sliced
2 10-3/4 oz. cans cream of
    mushroom soup

1-1/4 c. milk or water
1 onion, sliced and separated
    into rounds

Press uncooked beef into the bottom of an ungreased 13"x9" baking pan; season with salt and pepper. Arrange potato slices over beef; set aside. In a bowl, mix soup with milk or water; pour over potatoes. Arrange onion rounds on top; season again with salt and pepper. Cover with aluminum foil. Bake at 375 degrees for 30 minutes; remove foil and bake another 30 to 35 minutes. Makes 6 to 8 servings.

Gourds and mini pumpkins left over from Halloween can do double duty on the Thanksgiving table. Spray them gold or glittery with craft paint and tuck into harvest centerpieces.

Back-to-School FALL RECIPES

Crispy Fish Nuggets

Laura Fuller
Fort Wayne, IN

We've been trying to eat fish more often at our house.
The kids love these crispy nuggets!

1 c. panko bread crumbs
1 T. fresh thyme, chopped
1/2 c. all-purpose flour
1/2 t. salt
1/2 t. pepper
1 egg, lightly beaten

2 T. water
1-1/2 lbs. cod fillets, thawed
  if frozen and cubed
Garnish: tartar sauce or
  cocktail sauce

Heat a skillet over medium-high heat; add panko and thyme. Cook for about 2 minutes, stirring often, until golden. Transfer panko mixture to a shallow dish; place flour, salt and pepper in another shallow dish. Whisk together egg and water in a third shallow dish. Coat fish in flour mixture; dip into egg mixture and coat well in panko mixture. Arrange fish in a single layer on a baking sheet coated with non-stick vegetable spray. Bake at 400 degrees for 12 minutes, or until golden and fish flakes easily. Drain on paper towels; serve with sauce for dipping. Makes 4 servings.

Mix up a quick tartar sauce for fish. Combine 1/2 cup mayonnaise, 2 tablespoons sweet pickle relish and one tablespoon lemon juice. Chill until serving time.

FAMILY FAVORITES
for Dinnertime

Lemon Pasta With Broccoli

Paula Marchesi
Auburn, PA

I love to cook and bake, and have been doing so for well over 50 years. As a working mother of five boys, all in sports, I definitely needed something quick & easy to feed my family.

8-oz. pkg. angel hair pasta
   uncooked
2 cloves garlic, minced
2 T. butter
10-oz. pkg. frozen chopped
   broccoli, thawed

3 T. lemon juice
2 t. lemon zest
1/2 t. salt
1/4 t. pepper
Optional: grated Parmesan
   cheese

Cook pasta according to package directions; drain. Meanwhile, in a large skillet over medium heat, sauté garlic in butter until tender. Add broccoli, lemon juice and zest, salt and pepper. Cook for 3 to 5 minutes, until broccoli is crisp-tender. Add cooked pasta to skillet; toss to coat. Top with Parmesan cheese, if desired. Makes 6 servings.

Enjoy an evening of Halloween movies at home on a chilly autumn evening...fun for the whole family! Let the kids each invite a special friend and scatter plump cushions on the floor for extra seating. Pass the popcorn, please!

Back-to-School FALL RECIPES

Spinach & Ziti Pasta Bake

Jessica Kraus
Delaware, OH

This is a great, easy recipe that's good enough for company.
It's filling and delicious with a salad on the side.

1 lb. ziti pasta, uncooked
1 lb. ground beef
15-oz. jar marinara sauce
8-oz. container sour cream
1 t. Italian seasoning

salt and pepper to taste
10-oz. pkg. frozen chopped
 spinach, thawed and drained
1 c. shredded mozzarella cheese

Cook pasta according to package directions; drain. Meanwhile, crumble beef into a skillet over medium-high heat. Cook, stirring constantly, until evenly browned. Drain; stir in marinara sauce, sour cream and seasonings. Transfer cooked pasta to a greased 13"x9" baking pan; spoon beef mixture over pasta. Spread spinach over top; sprinkle with shredded cheese. Bake, uncovered, at 350 degrees for 30 minutes, or until heated through and lightly golden. Makes 8 servings.

Hosting a harvest potluck is one of my favorite things to do in the fall. Everyone brings a dish, and I make some sort of yummy-smelling main course, along with spiced cider in a simmering slow cooker. After dinner on our pergola, we carve pumpkins and have a cozy fire, with s'mores for dessert. It's a great way to share good food and good times with friends!

– Sheri Dulaney, Englewood, OH

FAMILY FAVORITES
for Dinnertime

No-Fuss Lasagna

Cindy Neel
Gooseberry Patch

An easy version of this get-together favorite...
you don't even have to boil the noodles!

1 lb. lean ground beef
4 c. tomato-basil pasta sauce
6 lasagna noodles, uncooked
15-oz. container ricotta cheese

8-oz. pkg. shredded mozzarella
   cheese
1/4 c. boiling water

Cook beef in a large skillet over medium heat until no longer pink.
Drain; stir in pasta sauce. Spread 1/3 of beef mixture in a lightly greased
11"x7" baking pan; layer with 3 noodles and 1/2 each of ricotta cheese
and mozzarella cheese. (Ricotta layers will be thin.) Repeat layering;
spread remaining 1/3 of beef mixture on top. Carefully pour boiling
water around inside edge of pan. Tightly cover with 2 layers of heavy-
duty aluminum foil. Bake at 375 degrees for 45 minutes; uncover and
bake 10 more minutes. Let stand 10 minutes; cut into squares.
Makes 6 to 8 servings.

Easy Stuffed Shells

Geneva Rogers
Gillette, WY

This is potluck-friendly and you can use your favorite flavor of
pasta sauce. My kids like to help put the meatballs in the shells!

24 jumbo pasta shells, uncooked
24-oz. jar spaghetti sauce,
   divided
24 frozen Italian meatballs,
   thawed

8-oz. pkg. shredded
   mozzarella cheese

Cook pasta shells according to package directions; drain and rinse in
cold water. Spread 1/2 cup sauce in a greased 13"x9" baking pan. Tuck
a meatball into each shell; arrange shells over sauce. Top with remaining
sauce and cheese. Cover and bake at 350 degrees for 35 minutes.
Uncover and bake another 3 to 5 minutes, until bubbly and cheese
is melted. Let stand several minutes before serving. Makes 8 to
12 servings.

Back-to-School
FALL RECIPES

Shredded Ham Sandwiches

Lynn Williams
Muncie, IN

My boys play high school football, so they're always hungry! I love how easy slow-cooker sandwiches are to fix for them and their friends. This is a delicious change from pulled pork.

2 12-oz. bottles regular or
   non-alcoholic beer
1/2 c. German or Dijon mustard,
   divided
1/2 t. pepper

4-lb. fully cooked bone-in ham
4 fresh rosemary sprigs
15 pretzel buns, split
Garnish: additional mustard,
   dill pickle slices

In a 5-quart slow cooker, whisk together beer, mustard and pepper. Add ham to slow cooker; top with rosemary sprigs. Cover and cook on low setting for 7 to 9 hours, until ham is tender. Remove ham to a platter; cool slightly. Discard rosemary sprigs; skim fat from cooking juices. Shred ham with 2 forks; discard bone. Return ham to juices in slow cooker; heat through. To serve, fill buns with shredded ham, using tongs. Top with mustard and pickle slices. Makes 15 sandwiches.

There's always room for one more at the Thanksgiving table. Why not invite a neighbor or a college student who might be spending the holiday alone to share your feast?

FAMILY FAVORITES
for Dinnertime

Roasted Italian Sausages, Peppers & Potatoes

Marcia Shaffer
Conneaut Lake, PA

This is a delicious all-in-one meal that's so easy! Serve the sausages on buns or alongside the roasted vegetables.

4 to 5 sweet or hot Italian pork
    sausage links
4 baking potatoes, peeled and
    quartered

2 green peppers, cut into strips
2 yellow onions, cut into strips
1 lb. mushrooms, quartered

Arrange sausage links and potatoes on a greased 15"x10" jelly-roll pan. Bake at 400 degrees for 30 minutes, turning sausages several times, or until lightly golden. Add vegetables to pan. Continue baking another 45 minutes, turning all occasionally, or until potatoes are tender and golden. Makes 4 to 5 servings.

Pork & Rice Casserole

Lisa Cunningham
Boothbay, ME

This is an easy and delicious recipe, using just a few ingredients. It's perfect for a busy weeknight...great for entertaining guests, too! Serve with crusty rolls and a tossed salad.

4 thick boneless pork chops
1 T. oil
3/4 c. instant rice, uncooked
1-oz. pkg. onion soup mix

2 10-3/4 oz. cans cream of
    mushroom soup
2-1/2 c. water

In a large skillet over medium heat, brown pork chops in oil; drain. Spread rice in a greased 13"x9" baking pan; arrange browned chops on top. Sprinkle soup mix over chops. In a bowl, whisk together soup and water; spoon over top. Cover pan tightly with aluminum foil. Bake at 350 degrees for 45 to 60 minutes. Makes 4 servings.

Back-to-School
FALL RECIPES

Not Your Momma's Fish Patties

Beckie Apple
Grannis, AR

My mother used to make fish patties for us when I was a kid and we loved them. I began experimenting using half tuna and half chicken. We really like them, because it makes for a lighter fish flavor, which my family prefers. Be careful, you can eat these as fast as you fry them! For an excellent sandwich, make the patties bun-size. Serve with mayonnaise or tartar sauce.

6-oz. can tuna, drained
5-oz. can chunk white chicken,
  flaked
1 egg, beaten
1 T. milk

1-1/2 t. minced, dried onion
1/8 t. salt
1/4 t. pepper
3 T. self-rising flour
oil for frying

In a bowl, combine drained tuna and undrained chicken; mash well with a fork. In another bowl, whisk together egg, milk, onion and seasonings. Stir in flour; add tuna mixture and mix well. In a skillet over medium heat, heat one teaspoon oil. Add tuna mixture, 2 tablespoons per patty, placing 2 inches apart. Cook for one to 1-1/2 minutes; turn over and cook until golden on other side. Continue with remaining tuna mixture, adding a little oil to skillet each time. Drain patties on paper towels; serve hot. Makes 6 servings.

Make a simple, kid-friendly side that's ready to serve in a jiffy! Cook a package of thin spaghetti and toss with a little butter and grated Parmesan cheese. Or try chopped tomato and a drizzle of olive oil...equally quick and tasty.

FAMILY FAVORITES
for Dinnertime

Chicken Ranch Sandwiches

*Mel Chencharick
Julian, PA*

Quick and delicious...what more could you ask for? A slow cooker makes it easy. These are great for a take-along dish.

4 boneless, skinless chicken
  breasts
8-oz. pkg. cream cheese,
  softened
1-oz. pkg. buttermilk ranch
  salad dressing mix
8-oz. pkg. shredded mild or
  sharp Cheddar cheese

8 slices bacon, crisply cooked
  and crumbled
8 hamburger buns, split
Optional: 2 green onions,
  chopped

Layer chicken breasts in a 4-quart slow cooker. Top chicken with cream cheese; sprinkle with dressing mix. Cover and cook on low setting for 6 hours, or until chicken is very tender. Shred chicken mixture in the slow cooker, using 2 forks. Sprinkle cheese and bacon over chicken. Cover for about 15 minutes, just until cheese is melted. To serve, spoon chicken mixture onto buns; sprinkle with onions, if desired. Makes 8 sandwiches.

Jazz up the Thanksgiving leftovers...try stuffing waffles! To 2 cups leftover stuffing, add an egg and enough chicken broth to moisten. Bake in a waffle maker, using 1/2 cup per waffle. Serve hot waffles topped with mashed potatoes, turkey and a drizzle of gravy...yum!

Back-to-School
FALL RECIPES

Chicken Lasagna

Jill Arends
Estherville, IA

When our youngest son played football, every Thursday after practice we served a "pasta feed" for the team. This was their favorite pasta and it's so easy to make. With French bread and a tossed salad on the side, we had a quick & easy meal for a crowd.

12 lasagna noodles, uncooked
4 c. cooked chicken, cubed
10-3/4 oz. can cream of chicken
   soup
10-3/4 oz. can cream of celery
   soup
3/4 c. sour cream

1/2 c. mayonnaise
4-oz. can sliced black olives,
   drained
8-oz. pkg. shredded Cheddar
   cheese, divided
1/2 c. grated Parmesan cheese

Cook noodles according to package directions; drain. Meanwhile, in a large bowl, combine chicken, soups, sour cream, mayonnaise, olives and one cup Cheddar cheese; mix well. In a greased 13"x9" baking pan, layer 4 noodles and 1/3 of chicken mixture; repeat twice. Top with Parmesan cheese and remaining Cheddar cheese. Cover and bake at 350 degrees for 30 minutes. Uncover; bake for another 15 to 30 minutes, until bubbly and cheese is melted. Let stand for 10 minutes; cut into squares. Serves 12.

Make a scarecrow with the children! Nail together long and short posts in a T-shape. Dress your scarecrow in a straw-stuffed old shirt and pants and add a pumpkin or a stuffed paper bag for a head. Sure to be fun!

FAMILY FAVORITES
for Dinnertime

Ranch-Style Casserole

Caroline Timbs
Cord, AR

I grew up eating this yummy casserole...I've never tasted
another enchilada-style casserole quite like it!

1 lb. ground beef
1 onion, diced
8 corn tortillas, divided
15-oz. can ranch-style beans
10-3/4 oz. can cream of
    mushroom soup
10-oz. can enchilada sauce

4-oz. can sliced black olives,
    drained
4-oz. can sliced mushrooms,
    drained
8-oz. pkg. shredded Mexican-
    style cheese, divided

In a skillet over medium heat, brown beef with onion; drain. In a
buttered 13"x9" baking pan, arrange 4 tortillas; set aside. In a large
bowl, combine remaining ingredients, setting aside one cup cheese for
topping. Spread half of beef mixture over tortillas. Top with 4 more corn
tortillas; add remaining beef mixture. Spread reserved cheese on top.
Cover with aluminum foil. Bake at 350 degrees for 45 minutes. Remove
foil; bake another 15 minutes, or until bubbly and cheese is melted.
Makes 8 to 10 servings.

Hosting a crowd for dinner? Serve festive Mexican or Italian
dishes that everybody loves. They usually feature rice or pasta,
so they're filling yet budget-friendly. The theme makes it a
snap to put together the menu and table decorations too.

Back-to-School
FALL RECIPES

Sweet & Spicy Pork Sandwiches *Devi McDonald*
Visalia, CA

*Our family loves coming up with new and interesting sandwich
ideas and this one is one of our favorites. It's a little sweet,
a little spicy and really delicious! So simple in a slow cooker.*

1 onion, sliced 1/2-inch thick
4 cloves garlic, pressed
2-1/2 lb. pork loin roast
1 t. smoked paprika
1 t. salt
1 t. pepper

1/2 c. sliced yellow pepperoncini,
   drained
1 c. root beer
1/2 c. beef broth
3 T. honey
8 to 10 sandwich buns, split

Place onion and garlic in a slow cooker. Rub roast with seasonings; add
to slow cooker. Top roast with peppers; drizzle with root beer, broth and
honey. Cover and cook on low setting for 8 hours, or until pork shreds
easily. Serve on buns. Makes 8 to 10 sandwiches.

My most favorite memories of fall are chilly fall evenings
in Wyoming. I would drive back home on the weekends from
college and couldn't wait to get on my horse and ride. One of
the most beautiful places to ride was along the Laramie River.
The trees were gorgeous and the air was crisp. I can still
hear the sound of the leaves crackling under my horse's
hooves. Such wonderful fall memories!

– Brittney Green, Frederick, CO

FAMILY FAVORITES
for Dinnertime

Bar-B-Q Beef Sandwiches

Sue Avilio
Bayville, NJ

We make this slow-cooker recipe every year for our
harvest party in the fall. My family absolutely loves it!

1-1/2 lbs. beef top round steak
   or London broil, cut into
   3-inch cubes and fat trimmed
1/2 t. salt
1/4 t. pepper
2 c. shredded coleslaw mix
1/2 c. onion, coarsely chopped

1/4 c. long-grain rice, uncooked
1/2 c. barbecue sauce
1/2 c. water
8 sandwich buns, split
Optional: 8 slices Colby-Jack
   cheese

Season beef cubes with salt and pepper; set aside. In a bowl, combine coleslaw mix, onion, rice, barbecue sauce and water. In a 4-quart slow cooker, layer beef cubes and coleslaw mixture. Cover and cook on low setting for about 8 hours, until beef shreds easily. Fill buns with beef mixture; top with a slice of cheese, if desired. Makes 8 sandwiches.

A child should always say what's true
And speak when he is spoken to,
And behave mannerly at table;
At least as far as he is able.

– Robert Louis Stevenson

119

Back-to-School
FALL RECIPES

Pepper Jack Chicken

Julie Dossantos
Fort Pierce, FL

This is a twist on a family favorite, Swiss chicken. It's a simple main dish that's delicious served over hot cooked rice. A spoonful of sour cream adds a cool contrast to the heat in the salsa and cheese.

4 boneless, skinless chicken breasts
4 slices Pepper Jack cheese
1 c. favorite salsa
1 c. tortilla chips, crushed
hot cooked rice
Optional: sour cream

Arrange chicken in a lightly greased 3-quart casserole dish. Top each piece of chicken with one cheese slice; spoon salsa over top. Cover and bake at 350 degrees for 30 minutes. Uncover; sprinkle crushed chips over chicken. Cook an additional 10 to 15 minutes, until chicken is no longer pink in the center. Serve over cooked rice, topped with sour cream, if desired. Makes 4 servings.

Make some autumn placemats with leaf rubbings...
fun for kids! Arrange leaves face-down on plain white
paper and cover with another sheet of paper. Unwrap
crayons and rub them over the leaves. Their images
will magically appear.

PIZZAS, BURGERS, Dogs & Tacos

Back-to-School
FALL RECIPES

Brianna's Pizza Pasta

Lee Beedle
Martinsburg, WV

One day, my nine-year-old daughter Brianna came rushing home from school to tell me she had a new recipe. When I asked where she got the recipe, she replied, "I asked the cooks in the cafeteria at school for it." That's my girl!

16-oz. pkg. elbow macaroni or
  rotini pasta, uncooked
1/2 lb. ground beef
1/2 lb. sweet basil pork sausage
  links, casings removed
1/2 lb. sliced mushrooms

3 15-oz. jars pizza sauce
5-oz. pkg. mini pepperoni slices
8-oz. pkg. shredded pizza-blend
  or mozzarella cheese, divided
Optional: other favorite pizza
  toppings

Cook macaroni or pasta according to package directions; drain. Meanwhile, in a skillet over medium heat, cook beef with sausage. When almost done, add mushrooms; cook until browned. Drain; transfer beef mixture to a large bowl. Add macaroni, pizza sauce, pepperoni, half the cheese and any optional toppings; mix thoroughly. Transfer to a 13"x9" baking pan coated with non-stick vegetable spray. Sprinkle remaining cheese on top. Cover and bake at 325 degrees for 20 minutes. Uncover and bake an additional 5 minutes, or bubbly and until cheese is lightly golden. Makes 6 to 8 servings.

If lots of kids are coming over for an after-game party, make dinnertime easy! Set out the toppings for do-it-yourself tacos, mini pizzas or hot dogs...guests can fix theirs just the way they like. Round out the menu with pitchers of lemonade and a yummy dessert pizza. Simple and fun!

PIZZAS, BURGERS, Dogs & Tacos

Garden-To-Table Spinach-Alfredo Pizza

Amy Thomason Hunt
Traphill, NC

This is a must on my farmhouse table whenever my best friend Sue comes for a visit. I think you'll love it too!

6-1/2 oz. pkg. pizza crust mix
1/2 to 3/4 c. basil and garlic
   Alfredo sauce
4 c. fresh spinach, chopped
2 tomatoes, diced

1/2 c. sliced mushrooms
1/2 c. red onion, diced
8-oz. pkg. shredded pizza-blend
   cheese

Prepare crust mix according to package directions. Spread dough on a 12" round pizza pan coated with non-stick vegetable spray. Spread Alfredo sauce over dough, leaving a one-inch edge. Top with spinach, tomatoes, mushrooms and onion; sprinkle with cheese. Bake at 450 degrees for 10 to 15 minutes, until cheese is melted and crust is golden. Let stand for several minutes; cut into wedges or squares. Makes 4 to 6 servings.

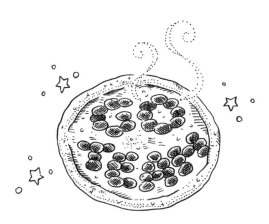

October is National Pizza Month, so treat game-day fans to homemade pizza for dinner. You can even spell out the team's name in pepperoni! Serve with plates, cutlery and napkins in team colors...fun for everyone!

Back-to-School
FALL RECIPES

Bacon Cheeseburger Pizza

Carolyn Deckard
Bedford, IN

This pizza is one of my grandkids' favorites. I always keep everything on hand to make this pizza when they come for a visit.

10-oz. tube refrigerated pizza
  dough
1/2 lb. lean ground beef
1/2 c. onion, chopped
8-oz. can pizza sauce

1 tomato, thinly sliced
2 slices bacon, crisply cooked
  and crumbled
1 c. shredded Cheddar cheese or
  diced American cheese

Unroll pizza dough according to package directions. Place on a greased baking sheet; build up edges slightly. Bake at 425 degrees for 8 to 10 minutes, until lightly golden. Meanwhile, in a large skillet over medium heat, cook beef and onion until beef is browned and onion is tender. Drain well. Spread pizza sauce over hot crust; spoon beef mixture over sauce. Top with tomato slices and bacon pieces; sprinkle with cheese. Bake at 425 degrees for about 10 minutes, or until sauce is bubbly and cheese is melted. Let stand several minutes; cut into squares. Makes 4 servings.

Prefer to shred cheese yourself? Place the wrapped block of cheese in the freezer for 15 minutes...it will just glide across the grater! Use right away, or refrigerate in a plastic zipping bag up to 3 days. An 8-ounce package of shredded cheese is about 2 cups.

124

PIZZAS, BURGERS,
Dogs & Tacos

Nana's Taco Casserole

Tina Hennessy
Flower Mound, TX

When I got married more than 30 years ago, my mom gave me a recipe book. This recipe was in it...it has been one of my family's favorites all those years.

16-oz. pkg wide egg noodles, uncooked
1 lb. ground beef
1 to 1-1/2 1-oz. pkgs. taco seasoning mix, to taste
3/4 c. water
2 14-1/2 oz. cans stewed tomatoes
3 c. shredded Cheddar cheese

Cook egg noodles according to package directions; drain. Meanwhile, cook beef in a large skillet over medium heat; drain. Stir in taco seasoning and water; reduce heat to medium-low. Cover and simmer for 10 minutes, stirring occasionally. Add stewed tomatoes with juice; gently mix noodles into beef mixture. Transfer to a greased 13"x9" baking pan; cover with cheese. Bake at 350 degrees for 20 minutes. Makes 6 to 8 servings.

Every September, we have fun looking at the calendar and planning our first "Friday by the Fire"! Even though we live in Florida and fall is usually quite warm, our family loves to usher in each season and enjoy the special moments that we can share. In October, shortly before Halloween, we plan a Friday night around the fire pit. We prepare a fun meal together and always have s'mores for dessert! This special evening is repeated often during the following months.

– Muriel Vlahakis, Sarasota, FL

Back-to-School
FALL RECIPES

Easiest-Ever Chicken Tacos

Joann Kurtz
Wichita Falls, TX

This slow-cooker recipe came from my daughter-in-law. You can add more chicken and use it for chicken enchiladas, nachos or whatever tickles your fancy...easy and delicious!

4 to 6 boneless, skinless
   chicken breasts
2 t. dried cumin
16-oz. jar mild salsa verde
16-oz. jar medium salsa verde

12 8-inch flour tortillas
Garnish: shredded Cheddar
   cheese, sour cream, salsa,
   shredded lettuce, diced
   tomatoes

Place chicken in a 5-quart slow cooker. Sprinkle with cumin; pour salsa over top. Cover and cook on low setting for 6 hours, or until chicken is very tender. Remove chicken to a plate; shred with 2 forks. Fill tortillas with chicken. Set out condiments and let everyone fix their tacos just the way they like them. Serves 4 to 6.

Southwestern Beef Tacos

Joanna Nicoline-Haughey
Berwyn, PA

This is super-easy to toss together...I like to serve it with a side of cornbread. To spice it up, use medium to hot salsa.

1 lb. ground beef
15-1/2 oz. can black beans,
   drained and rinsed
11-oz. can sweet corn and
   diced peppers, drained

1-1/2 c. favorite salsa
12 hard corn taco shells
Garnish: sour cream, chopped
   lettuce, diced tomatoes

Brown beef in a skillet over medium heat; drain. Stir in beans, corn and salsa. Cover and simmer over medium-low heat for 10 minutes, stirring occasionally. Heat taco shells in a 350-degree oven for 5 minutes. Spoon beef mixture into taco shells; garnish as desired. Makes 4 servings, 3 tacos each.

If kids find tacos hard to handle, serve 'em taco dogs instead!
Just spoon fillings into a hot dog bun and serve.

126

PIZZAS, BURGERS, *Dogs & Tacos*

Yellow Squash Tacos

Brianna Cooper-Risser
Mount Vernon, OH

After growing weary of stir-fry, our family tried substituting yellow summer squash for beef in our tacos...the results were delicious! You can also use the leftovers to make quesadillas.

1 to 2 yellow squash, diced
4 t. oil, divided
1-oz. pkg. taco seasoning mix
1 c. water
1/2 red onion, diced
1 green pepper, diced
2 cloves garlic, chopped
8 hard corn taco shells
Garnish: shredded lettuce, sliced tomatoes, shredded Cheddar cheese

In a skillet over medium heat, sauté squash in 2 teaspoons oil. Stir in taco seasoning and water; simmer for 3 minutes. Meanwhile, in a separate skillet, sauté onion, green pepper and garlic in remaining oil until tender. Add onion mixture to squash mixture; simmer for 2 to 5 minutes. To serve, spoon squash mixture into taco shells; add desired toppings. Serves 4, 2 tacos each.

Shredded Pork Tacos

Mary Isom
Labadie, MO

One day, I had to work all day and did not want to come home and cook. I found a pork loin in the freezer and decided to try cooking it in my slow cooker. It came out yummy and my family loved it.

1-lb. pork loin
2 1-1/4 oz. pkgs. taco seasoning mix
1/2 c. water
8 to 10 8-inch flour tortillas
Garnish: shredded Mexican cheese, shredded lettuce, chopped tomatoes

Place pork loin in a 3-quart slow cooker. Mix taco seasoning with water; pour over pork loin. Cover and cook on low setting for 7 to 8 hours, until very tender. Using 2 forks, shred pork loin. Serve on tortillas; add desired toppings. Makes 8 to 10 servings.

Back-to-School
FALL RECIPES

Barbecued Hot Dogs

Andrea Ford
Montfort, WI

This sauce just takes a few minutes to put together, and it certainly makes hot dogs taste wonderful! It makes more than enough sauce for two packages of hot dogs.

1/2 c. onion, chopped
2 T. butter
1 c. catsup
1/2 c. water
1/4 c. lemon juice
3 T. Worcestershire sauce
2 T. brown sugar, packed

2 T. vinegar
1-1/2 t. mustard
1/2 t. salt
1/8 t. pepper
8 hot dogs
8 hot dog buns, split

In a saucepan over medium heat, sauté onion in butter. Add remaining ingredients except hot dogs and buns; simmer for 15 minutes. Arrange hot dogs in a lightly greased 13"x9" baking pan; spoon sauce over hot dogs. Bake, uncovered, at 350 degrees for 30 minutes. Serve hot dogs on buns, topped with sauce. Serves 8.

Southwest Turkey Burgers

Diane Cohen
Breinigsville, PA

This is our favorite recipe for turkey burgers...it's delicious!

1-1/2 lbs. lean ground turkey
1/4 c. shredded Pepper Jack or
   Cheddar cheese
2 T. soy sauce
2 T. garlic, minced
1 t. chili powder

1/4 c. plus 2 T. barbecue sauce,
   divided
1 sweet onion, thinly sliced
1 t. olive oil
4 sandwich buns, split and
   toasted

In a bowl, combine turkey, cheese, soy sauce, garlic, chili powder and 2 tablespoons barbecue sauce. Mix well; form into 4 patties. Place on a heated grill. Cook until internal temperature reaches 165 degrees, flipping once. Meanwhile, sauté onion in oil until soft and caramelized; stir in remaining barbecue sauce. Serve burgers on toasted buns, topped with onion mixture. Serves 4.

PIZZAS, BURGERS, Dogs & Tacos

Chili Cheese Dogs

Bootsie Dominick
Sandy Springs, GA

Who doesn't love a good chili cheese dog with chips?

1 lb. ground beef chuck
1 c. onion, chopped
1 t. garlic, minced
15-oz. can tomato sauce
1 c. water
2 T. chili powder, or to taste
1/4 t. salt
1/4 t. pepper
8 hot dogs, cooked
8 hot dog buns, split and toasted
Garnish: shredded Cheddar
  cheese

In a large skillet over medium heat, combine beef, onion and garlic. Cook until beef is browned; drain. Stir in tomato sauce, water and seasonings. Bring to a boil; reduce heat to medium-low. Cover and simmer for 25 minutes, stirring occasionally. To serve, spoon chili sauce over hot dogs in buns; top with cheese. Makes 8 servings.

To me, fall is the best season of the year! It has always been my favorite, even as a little girl. I love the leaves changing colors, the air getting cooler, wearing sweaters and jeans, football games, Honey Crisp apples, apple cider, hot chocolate...in other words, everything! When my grandchildren were younger, my son and daughter-in-law would host a Halloween party at their home for their neighborhood. My husband and I would help cook the hot dogs and other neighbors would bring various dishes. There would be a hayride and then trick-or-treating... what's not to like?

– Bootsie Dominick, Sandy Springs, GA

Back-to-School
FALL RECIPES

Open-Face Franks

Barbara Imler
Noblesville, IN

I used to make these for my children when they were growing up. They're similar to hot dogs on a bun, but different enough for the kids to think they're having something special.

6 hot dogs	1 T. dried, minced onion
2 T. mustard	1/2 t. dried oregano
Optional: 2 T. pickle relish	1/2 t. salt
1 c. all-purpose flour	1 egg
1/2 c. cornmeal	1/2 c. milk
2 t. sugar	3 T. butter, melted
1-1/2 t. baking powder	1/2 c. shredded Cheddar cheese

Cut hot dogs lengthwise, but not all the way through. Mix mustard and relish, if using; spread down the center of each hot dog. In a bowl, combine flour, cornmeal, sugar, baking powder, onion and seasonings. In a separate bowl, lightly beat together egg, milk and butter; add to flour mixture and beat until a soft dough forms. Spread dough in a greased 11"x7" baking pan. Arrange hot dogs, cut-side up, slightly apart down the length of the pan, pressing slightly into the dough. Sprinkle with cheese. Bake, uncovered, at 400 degrees for 25 to 30 minutes, until a toothpick inserted into crust comes out clean. To serve, slice crust between hot dogs. Makes 6 servings.

The beauty that shimmers in the yellow afternoons
of October, who could ever clutch it?
– Ralph Waldo Emerson

PIZZAS, BURGERS, *Dogs & Tacos*

Skillet Dogs & Potatoes

April Jacobs
Loveland, CO

This is a tasty one-pot meal! It takes a few simple ingredients and makes them more special. Try it with sliced smoked sausage too.

4 redskin potatoes, peeled and
   cubed
4 quarter-pound hot dogs
3 T. oil, divided

1 onion, chopped
1 red or green pepper, diced
1 t. dried sage
salt and pepper to taste

In a saucepan, cover potatoes with water. Bring to a boil over high heat; reduce heat to medium and cook until partially tender. Meanwhile, make shallow cuts in hot dogs once every inch, no more than halfway through. Heat one tablespoon oil in a large skillet over medium heat. Add hot dogs and cook for 5 minutes, or until browned, turning occasionally. Remove hot dogs to a plate. Add remaining oil, potatoes, onion and red or green pepper to skillet. Cook and stir for 12 to 15 minutes, until potatoes are golden. Sprinkle with seasonings; stir well. Return hot dogs to skillet. Cook until heated through, about 5 minutes, turning hot dogs once halfway through cooking time. Serves 4.

Whip up some back-to-school clipboards to show off the children's best artwork, bragging-rights school papers and other special items. Decorate dollar-store clipboards with paint, add each child's name with wooden game tiles and hang up the clipboards on nails...it's that simple.

Back-to-School
FALL RECIPES

Upside-Down Pizza

Kathy Courington
Canton, GA

Years ago, a friend served this when we visited her. I loved it so much, she told me the recipe and we have enjoyed it as a family ever since. Easy and so good for entertaining or a potluck.

1 lb. mild Italian ground
   pork sausage
3/4 c. onion, chopped
15-1/2 oz. jar pizza sauce
4-oz. sliced black olives, drained
4-oz. can sliced mushrooms,
   drained
2 to 3 c. shredded mozzarella
   cheese

2 eggs, beaten
1 c. milk
1 T. oil
1 c. all-purpose flour
1/4 t. salt
1/4 c. grated Parmesan cheese

In a skillet over medium heat, brown sausage with onion; drain. Add pizza sauce, olives and mushrooms; cook until bubbly and spoon into a greased 13"x9" baking pan. Spread mozzarella cheese evenly over top. Combine eggs, milk, oil, flour and salt in a blender; process until smooth (or stir together in a bowl). Pour batter over mozzarella cheese; sprinkle with Parmesan cheese. Bake, uncovered, at 400 degrees for about 30 minutes, until puffed and golden. Cut and serve immediately. Serves 6 to 8.

How spooky...mummy dogs! Simply wrap strips of bread stick dough around hot dogs. Arrange them on an ungreased baking sheet and bake at 375 degrees for 12 to 15 minutes, until golden. Add eyes with dots of catsup or mustard.

PIZZAS, BURGERS, Dogs & Tacos

Grandma Gigi's Pizza Sauce

Becky Bosen
Syracuse, UT

One day while making pizzas for my kids, I ran out of pizza sauce. So I created this recipe. My 13-year-old said it was the best pizza he'd ever eaten. That warmed my heart...I knew it was a keeper!

15-oz. can tomato sauce
3 cloves garlic, minced
1-1/4 t. dried, minced onion
1 t. sugar

1 t. Italian seasoning
1 t. dried basil
1/2 t. salt

Combine all ingredients in a small saucepan; mix well. Bring to a boil over medium-high heat. Reduce heat to low. Simmer for 20 minutes, stirring occasionally. Cool for 10 minutes before using. Makes about 2 cups.

Homemade Pizza Crust

Lori Peterson
Effingham, KS

This crust recipe of my mother's is still by far the best I have ever tasted! Growing up, it was such a treat to have homemade pizza. We got to pick our favorite toppings and put on as much cheese as we wanted. Now as an adult, I like to choose healthier toppings.

1/2 t. active dry yeast
3/4 c. very warm water, 110 to
115 degrees, divided

1 T. oil
1 T. sugar
2 c. all-purpose flour

In a large bowl, mix yeast, 1/2 cup very warm water and oil. Let stand until dissolved; stir in sugar. Add 2 cups flour; stir. Slowly add enough of remaining warm water to make a soft dough. Knead on a floured surface for several minutes. Place in a greased bowl; cover and let rise for 1-1/2 hours. Flatten dough by hand; place in a greased pizza pan or baking sheet. Pierce all over with a fork. Bake at 450 degrees for 5 minutes. Add sauce and toppings as desired; bake for an additional 20 to 30 minutes. Makes enough dough for one thick crust or 2 regular crusts.

Back-to-School
FALL RECIPES

English Muffin Pizzas

Vicki Crase
Riverside, OH

Just like we all remember from the school lunchroom! They're still a great little lunch or after-school snack. You can make each little pizza to taste, just as everyone likes it.

6 English muffins, split
1 c. pizza sauce
3-1/2 oz. pkg. sliced pepperoni
8-oz. pkg. shredded pizza-blend cheese
1/2 to 1 c. ground pork sausage, browned and drained

4-oz. can sliced mushrooms, drained
2-oz. can sliced black olives, drained
1 green pepper, diced
1/2 c. onion, diced

Place English muffin halves cut-side up on an ungreased baking sheet. Top each muffin half with one tablespoon pizza sauce, 4 pepperoni slices and 2 tablespoons shredded cheese. Add remaining ingredients as desired; cover with remaining cheese. Bake at 425 degrees for 5 minutes, or until cheese is melted and golden. Serves 6, 2 each.

Funny-face pizza snacks! Let the kids make faces on their English Muffin Pizzas with toppings like pepperoni and black olive "eyes," carrot curl "hair" and green pepper "smiles."

134

PIZZAS, BURGERS, *Dogs & Tacos*

Sausage-Stuffed Pizza Peppers

Dale Duncan
Waterloo, IA

*The whole family enjoys these peppers filled with
our favorite pizza flavors.*

1 lb. Italian ground pork sausage
3/4 c. onion, diced
2 c. cooked rice
1-1/2 c. pizza sauce
1/2 c. grated Parmesan cheese

1 t. Italian seasoning
salt and pepper to taste
6 green peppers, tops and
  seeds removed
6 slices mozzarella cheese

Brown sausage with onion in a skillet over medium heat; drain. Stir in cooked rice, pizza sauce and Parmesan cheese; add seasonings. Spoon stuffing into peppers; arrange in an ungreased 13"x9" baking pan. Add 1/2 inch of water to pan; cover with aluminum foil. Bake at 350 degrees for 30 to 40 minutes, until peppers are tender and filling is cooked through. Remove from oven; uncover and top each pepper with a cheese slice. Place under broiler for 2 to 3 minutes, until cheese is melted. Serves 6.

If youngsters turn up their noses at the taste of green sweet peppers, give yellow, orange or red peppers a try. Their flavor is much milder and the colors are appealing to kids.

Back-to-School
FALL RECIPES

Corn Dog Casserole

Judey Truitt
Harlan, KY

My son was a very picky eater and it was hard to find something to feed our family of seven. Everyone liked this dish...it's easy to make and there are never any leftovers!

2 T. butter
16 hot dogs, cut into bite-size
  pieces
1/3 c. onion, finely chopped
2 eggs, beaten
1-1/2 c. milk

2 T. honey or sugar
2 8-1/2 oz. pkgs. corn
  muffin mix
Optional: 1 c. shredded Cheddar
  cheese

Melt butter in a skillet over medium heat. Cook hot dogs and onion until lightly golden; set aside to cool. Meanwhile, in a large bowl, combine remaining ingredients; mix well until moistened. Stir in hot dog mixture. Pour batter into a greased 13"x9" baking pan. Bake, uncovered, at 400 degrees for 30 to 40 minutes, until a toothpick comes out clean. Cut into squares. Makes 12 servings.

Foil Dogs

Lisa Seckora
Chippewa Falls, WI

This is a recipe we made when I was a child whenever we went camping. That was over 50-plus years ago! Easy to make...fun to share and eat. Now, my granddaughter is having fun making it too.

1 c. hot dogs, chopped
1 egg, hard-boiled, peeled
  and chopped
1 c. shredded Cheddar cheese

1/4 c. pickle relish
1 T. mustard
2 drops Worcestershire sauce
4 hot dog buns, split

In a bowl, mix together all ingredients except buns. Spoon into buns; wrap each bun in aluminum foil. Bake at 400 degrees for 15 minutes. On a campfire or gas grill, cook over low coals/heat, turning often, for 20 minutes. Makes 4 servings.

PIZZAS, BURGERS, *Dogs & Tacos*

Western Burgers

Dawn Raskiewicz
Alliance, NE

I was looking for a new way to fix hamburgers and this is what I came up with. They are very tasty! Serve with French fries or potato chips for a quick and fun meal.

1 lb. 85% lean ground beef
2 eggs, beaten
1/2 c. dry bread crumbs
1 to 2 T. dried, minced onion
1-1/2 t. smoke-flavored
    cooking sauce
1/4 t. western-style steak sauce

1/4 t. pepper
garlic powder to taste
4 hamburger buns, split and
    warmed
Garnish: sliced tomatoes, onion,
    dill pickles, lettuce leaves,
    other condiments

In a large bowl, combine all ingredients except buns and garnish. Mix well and form into patties. Cook patties in a skillet over medium-high heat until browned on both sides and no longer pink in the center. Serve on hamburger buns. Set out condiments so everyone can fix their own burger to their liking. Makes 4 servings.

When you need to chill lots of bottles of soda or water, you'll find they chill more quickly on ice than in the refrigerator. Just add beverages to an ice-filled cooler or galvanized tub...you'll save valuable refrigerator space too!

Back-to-School
FALL RECIPES

Beans & Wieners Waikiki

Leah McGowen
Roseburg, OR

This tasty dish is great for barbecues, holiday get-togethers and potlucks. Serve it as either a main or a side dish.

20-oz. can pineapple slices,
    drained and juice reserved
2 T. butter
1/3 c. green pepper, coarsely
    chopped
1/4 c. onion, chopped

8 hot dogs, cut into chunks
2 T. vinegar
1 T. soy sauce
1/3 c. catsup
1/3 c. brown sugar, packed
15-oz. can pork & beans

Cut pineapple into chunks, reserving 3 or 4 rings for garnish; set aide. Melt butter in a skillet over medium heat. Sauté green pepper, onion, pineapple and hot dog chunks until golden; simmer for 5 minutes. Add reserved pineapple juice, vinegar, soy sauce, catsup and brown sugar; cook and stir until bubbly. Pour pork & beans into a lightly greased 13"x9" baking pan. Add pineapple mixture; stir gently to blend. Halve reserved pineapple slices; arrange on top. Bake, uncovered, at 350 degrees for 30 minutes, or until hot and bubbly. Serves 6.

A fireside cookout can be as near as your own backyard!
Gather family & friends and enjoy the crisp fall air. Play touch
football, toast marshmallows, tell ghost stories, jump into
a pile of leaves...be a kid again!

PIZZAS, BURGERS, Dogs & Tacos

Homemade Coney Sauce

Carolyn Deckard
Bedford, IN

This is our favorite coney sauce when we're camping and roasting hot dogs. So easy to make...better than store-bought.

1 c. catsup	2 T. mustard
1 c. tomato juice	2 t. dried oregano
6 T. sugar	2 bay leaves
6 T. vinegar	salt and pepper to taste

Combine all ingredients in a saucepan over medium heat. Simmer for 15 minutes, stirring occasionally. Discard bay leaves before serving. Makes 8 servings.

Teriyaki Burgers

Tina Wright
Atlanta, GA

So simple! For parties, I like to make 8 mini burgers and serve them on Hawaiian slider buns. Jut cut the pineapple slices into wedges.

1-1/2 lbs. ground beef	1/2 c. teriyaki sauce
1/2 t. salt	4 pineapple slices
1/2 t. pepper	4 hamburger buns, split

Form beef into 4 patties, 1/2-inch thick; season with salt and pepper. On a grill over medium-high heat, grill to desired doneness, 4 to 5 minutes per side. Brush with teriyaki sauce during the last 2 minutes of cooking. Grill pineapple for one to 2 minutes per side, brushing with sauce. Serve burgers in buns, topped with pineapple slices. Makes 4 servings.

Celebrate National Cheeseburger Day on September 18... easiest holiday ever!

Back-to-School
FALL RECIPES

Mediterranean Chicken, Spinach & Feta Pizza

Joslyn Hornstrom
Elgin, IL

So quick & easy! Any time you're in a hurry for a meal or snack, whip up this delicious pizza. It's a great use for leftover chicken too.

12-inch pre-baked pizza crust
2 to 3 t. olive oil
1/2 c. pesto sauce
1/2 c. fresh baby spinach
1 c. cooked chicken, chopped
1/4 c. crumbled feta cheese
1 green onion, sliced

1/4 c. sliced Kalamata or black
   olives
2 to 3 plum tomatoes, sliced
Italian seasoning to taste
1-1/2 c. shredded mozzarella
   cheese
2 T. grated Parmesan cheese

Place pizza crust on an ungreased baking sheet; brush crust with olive oil. Spread pesto sauce to within 1/2-inch of edge. Arrange spinach, chicken, cheese, onion and olives over sauce. Layer with tomato slices; sprinkle with Italian seasoning. Top all with cheeses. Bake at 450 degrees 10 to 12 minutes, until cheese is bubbly and lightly golden. Let stand a few minutes; cut into wedges. Serves 2 to 3.

To go with your homemade pizza, make a chopped salad...
no cutting board needed! Add all the salad fixings except
dressing to a big bowl, then roll a pizza cutter back & forth
over them. Drizzle with dressing and serve.

PIZZAS, BURGERS, *Dogs & Tacos*

Pizza Spaghetti

Jaden Timbs
Cord, AR

One evening while my mom was making our usual school night spaghetti, I told her my ideal spaghetti would be beef, sausage, pepperoni, mushrooms, olives and peppers. She said, "So, you want a supreme pizza in spaghetti form?" and our recipe was born. We've loved it ever since. Mom serves this with tossed salad, garlic toast and shredded fresh Parmesan cheese.

16-oz. pkg. angel hair pasta, uncooked
1 lb. ground beef
1 lb. ground pork breakfast sausage
8-oz. container sliced mushrooms
1 onion, chopped
1 green pepper, chopped
3-1/2 oz. pkg. sliced pepperoni
2 24-oz. jars mushroom & pepper spaghetti sauce
2 4-oz. cans sliced black olives, drained

Cook pasta according to package directions; drain. Meanwhile, in a large, deep skillet over medium heat, brown beef and sausage. Drain and set aside; add mushrooms, onion and pepper to skillet. Sauté until tender; stir in beef mixture, pepperoni and pasta sauce. Reduce heat to low; heat through. Add olives and cooked pasta; stir to mix well. Makes 8 servings.

What feeling is so nice as a child's hand in yours?
So small, so soft and warm like a kitten huddling
in the shelter of your clasp.
– Marjorie Holmes

Back-to-School
FALL RECIPES

Chicken Veggie Burgers

Michelle Taggart
Castle Rock, CO

My family loves these burgers! I created this recipe when I found the ground chicken and turkey just needed a little help flavor-wise.

1 lb. ground chicken or turkey
1/4 c. carrot, peeled and finely
   chopped
1/4 c. onion, finely chopped
1 clove garlic, minced
1/2 c. zucchini or yellow squash,
   finely chopped

1/4 c. green or red pepper,
   finely chopped
1 t. ground cumin
1/2 t. ground coriander
1/2 t. dry mustard
4 hamburger buns, split

In a large bowl, combine all ingredients except buns; mix well and shape into 4 patties. On a skillet coated with non-stick vegetable spray, cook over medium heat, about 5 minutes on the first side and 3 minutes on the other. Finish cooking over low heat, about 5 minutes. Serve patties on buns. Makes 4 servings.

Marcie's Rosemary Turkey Burgers

Leona Krivda
Belle Vernon, PA

I got this recipe from my daughter. She is a great cook and we have all enjoyed these...they're very flavorful.

1/2 c. mayonnaise
1/4 c. fresh rosemary, chopped
2 T. garlic, minced
1 lb. ground turkey

4 hamburger buns, split and
   lightly toasted
Garnish: lettuce leaves,
   tomato slices

Combine mayonnaise, rosemary and garlic in a cup. Mix very well and set aside half of mixture. In a bowl, combine remaining mayonnaise mixture with turkey; mix well and form into 4 patties. Grill over low heat for about 10 minutes on each side. To serve, brush buns with reserved mayonnaise mixture; add burgers to buns. Garnish with lettuce and tomato. Makes 4 servings.

PIZZAS, BURGERS, Dogs & Tacos

Double Bacon Cheeseburgers

Wendy Meadows
Spring Hill, FL

My kids love these burgers and request them for their birthday dinners. We serve them with potato salad and baked beans.

1 lb. hickory-smoked bacon, divided
2 lbs. lean ground beef
3/4 c. onion, finely diced
2 T. Worcestershire sauce

1 c. shredded Cheddar cheese
6 slices Cheddar cheese
6 hamburger buns, split and toasted
Garnish: favorite burger toppings

In a skillet over medium heat, cook half of bacon slices until crisp; set aside to drain on paper towels. Meanwhile, finely chop remaining bacon; place in a bowl. Add beef, onion, Worcestershire sauce and cheese. Mix well and shape into 6 patties. On a grill over low to medium heat, grill on both sides until nearly done. Break crisp bacon slices in half; top each burger with 2 to 4 pieces bacon and a cheese slice. Cook until cheese completely melts. Assemble burgers on buns, adding desired toppings. Makes 6 servings.

The promise of a favorite meal can be all it takes to get kids motivated for a service project! The little time it takes to help weed a neighbor's garden or plant flowers around the school pays big rewards...kids learn to give of their time and care for others.

143

Back-to-School
FALL RECIPES

Pizza Burgers

Beverley Williams
San Antonio, TX

One day, my children were fussing over whether we should have
pizza or burgers. I settled the argument by making these!

1-1/2 lbs. ground beef
1/4 lb. ground pork Italian
  sausage
10 pepperoni slices, finely
  chopped
1/2 c. plus 2 T. pizza sauce,
  divided

6 slices mozzarella cheese
6 hamburger buns, split
Optional: sliced onions, green
  peppers, black olives,
  mushrooms

In a large bowl, combine beef, sausage, pepperoni and 1/2 cup pizza
sauce. Mix very well; form into 6 patties. Cook patties to desired
doneness on a grill or in a skillet; top each patty with a slice of cheese.
Spread remaining pizza sauce on cut sides of buns. Place patties on
buns; garnish as desired. Serves 6.

Beef & Bean Pizza Burgers

Amy Theisen
Sauk Rapids, MN

A quick & easy delicious meal at any time of year! These
open-face sandwiches are tasty on French bread too.

1 lb. ground beef
1/2 c. onion, chopped
6-oz. can tomato paste
3/4 c. canned black beans,
  drained and rinsed
1 t. dried oregano
1/2 t. garlic powder

1 t. salt
8 to 10 English muffins or
  sandwich buns, split
  and toasted
Garnish: shredded mozzarella
  cheese

Brown beef and onion in a skillet over medium heat. Drain; stir in
tomato paste, beans and seasonings. Simmer over medium-low heat for
15 minutes. Arrange muffin or bun halves on a baking sheet. Top with
beef mixture and desired amount of cheese. Broil for 2 to 3 minutes,
until cheese melts. Makes 8 to 10 servings.

PIZZAS, BURGERS, Dogs & Tacos

Hot Dogs Delicious

Nancy Christensen
West Des Moines, IA

These hot dogs were a favorite of our children, way back in the mid-1960s and 1970s. They're still a treat!

1/2 c. onion, chopped	1 T. vinegar
1 T. oil	1/4 t. salt
1/4 c. catsup	8 hot dogs
2 T. sweet or dill pickle relish	8 hot dog buns, split
1 T. sugar	

In a skillet over medium heat, cook onion in oil until golden. Add catsup, relish, sugar, vinegar and salt; stir well. Make several shallow cuts around hot dogs and add to sauce; simmer until heated through. Serve hot dogs on buns, topped with sauce. Makes 8 servings.

Way back in the mid-1950s, I loved it when my mom took me shopping for new school clothes each fall. She was a rarity in our neighborhood back then, as she had a career and wasn't often home during the day like other moms. When we shopped, it was really a big deal, as I was usually the recipient of my older sister's hand-me-downs. What I remember most were the special plaid hair ribbons Mom would buy for my outfits. When the first day of school arrived, a perfect pair of plaid ribbons was carefully ironed and laid out with my new dresses. Fall was a time of back-to-school, saddle oxfords and my new plaid ribbons... sweet memories!

– Hilary Milner, Simi Valley, CA

Back-to-School
FALL RECIPES

Brian's Taco Pie

Sandra Parker
Glen Burnie, MD

This was my son's favorite meal...he could practically eat the whole thing by himself! He would bring his friends home just to eat this taco pie with him.

9-inch deep-dish pie crust,
   unbaked
5 russet baking potatoes,
   peeled and cubed
1 lb. ground beef
1-1/4 oz. pkg. taco
   seasoning mix
3/4 c. water

1/2 c. milk
3 T. butter
1 t. garlic powder
salt and pepper to taste
1 c. shredded Pepper Jack cheese
1 c. shredded Cheddar cheese
Garnish: sour cream, sliced green
   onions

Bake pie crust according to package directions; set aside. In a large saucepan, cover potatoes with water; bring to a boil over high heat. Cook for 15 minutes, or until fork-tender; drain. Meanwhile, in a skillet over medium heat, brown beef and drain well. Stir in taco seasoning and water; simmer for several minutes. To cooked potatoes, add milk, butter and seasonings; mash well and set aside. Spoon beef mixture into pie crust; top with Pepper Jack cheese. Spread mashed potatoes on top; sprinkle with Cheddar cheese. Bake, uncovered, at 400 degrees for about 15 minutes, until bubbly and cheese is melted. Cut into wedges; serve topped with sour cream and onions. Makes 4 to 6 servings.

Make your own taco seasoning mix. In a jar, combine 3/4 cup dried, minced onion; 1/4 cup each salt and chili powder; 2 tablespoons each cornstarch, red pepper flakes, ground cumin and dried, minced garlic; and one tablespoon dried oregano. Four tablespoons of mix equals a 1-1/4 ounce envelope.

PIZZAS, BURGERS, Dogs & Tacos

Steakhouse Burgers with Mushroom Sauce

Connie Hilty
Pearland, TX

When I was growing up, this recipe was Dad's specialty whenever we had a cookout. We loved it! Now I fix these burgers for him on his birthday and Fathers' Day. They're still scrumptious.

1-1/2 lbs. ground beef
1/4 c. onion, grated
2 T. red steak sauce
1 T. fresh parsley, snipped
1 t. lemon zest

1 t. seasoned salt
1/4 t. pepper
6 Kaiser rolls, split
Garnish: sliced tomato, romaine
    lettuce, chopped fresh chives

In a large bowl, combine all ingredients except rolls and garnish. Mix well; shape into 6 patties, about 3/4-inch thick. Grill over medium-hot coals for 8 to 10 minutes on each side. To serve, place in rolls. Top with lettuce, tomato, a spoonful of Mushroom Sauce and a sprinkle of chives. Makes 6 servings.

Mushroom Sauce:

8-oz. container sliced
    mushrooms

3 T. butter
2 t. Dijon mustard

In a skillet over medium heat, sauté mushrooms in butter until tender and liquid is evaporated. Stir in mustard.

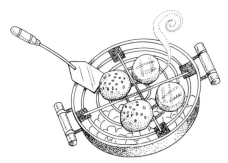

Burger buns just taste better toasted...and they won't get soggy! Butter buns lightly and place them on a hot grill for 30 seconds to one minute on each side, until toasty.

Back-to-School
FALL RECIPES

Black Beans & Rice

Kristen Lewis
Bourbonnais, IL

This is a quick & easy meatless skillet meal. Great spooned into taco shells and topped with sour cream, lettuce and cheese too.

15-oz. can low-sodium black
   beans, drained and rinsed
1-1/4 oz. pkg salt-free taco
   seasoning mix
3/4 c. water
1/2 green pepper, diced

1/2 yellow, red or orange pepper,
   diced
1/2 c. white onion, chopped
1 roma tomato, chopped
1 T. garlic, minced
3/4 c. cooked brown rice

In a skillet over medium heat, combine beans, taco seasoning and water. Stir in peppers and onion; cook until vegetables are soft. Add tomato and garlic. Cook about 3 minutes, until tomatoes are warmed. Stir in cooked rice; heat through and serve. Serves 4.

Florida Fish Tacos

Kendall Hale
Lynn, MA

We tried these on a family vacation and just had to try making them at home! Cod and halibut fillets are delicious too.

2 t. salt
2 t. cayenne pepper
1 t. pepper
6 4-oz. tilapia fillets,
   thawed if frozen

2 T. olive oil
12 8-inch corn tortillas, warmed
Garnish: corn salsa, sour cream,
   shredded cabbage

Combine seasonings on a plate. Brush fillets with oil; coat with spices. Arrange fillets on an oiled grill pan over medium-high heat. Cook for 3 minutes per side, or until golden and fish flakes easily. Fill tortillas with fish and desired toppings. Serves 6, 2 tacos each.

Vintage turkey salt & pepper
shakers brighten any
autumn tabletop.

PIZZAS, BURGERS, Dogs & Tacos

Fridge Fest Quesadillas

Barbara Imler
Noblesville, IN

This is a great way to use up leftovers. My husband loves it, and so will your family! We're retired and always have leftovers from our meals taking up space in the fridge. Every now & then, I'll take out those containers and use the contents to make quesadillas. My husband thinks they're a special treat...he has no idea he's eating leftovers!

2 10-inch flour tortillas
1/2 c. cooked vegetables, chopped
1/2 c. cooked meat, chopped

3/4 c. favorite shredded cheese
Garnish: jalapeño pepper slices, sour cream, salsa

Add one tortilla to a lightly greased skillet over medium heat. Scatter vegetables, meat and cheese over tortilla; top with second tortilla. Cook until golden on the bottom; flip carefully and cook until the other side is golden. Cut into quarters with a pizza cutter. Serve with jalapeños, sour cream and salsa, as desired. Serves one.

For meat: Leftover beef pot roast and pork roast are good, as are barbecued pork ribs and cooked chicken, turkey or shrimp. You may instead use chopped deli meat.

For vegetables: Corn is especially good. Cooked green beans, squash, carrots and even beets work well. Chopped fresh red or green pepper, onion and celery can also be added. Potatoes or other mushy vegetables don't work very well.

For authentic restaurant-style taco meat, brown ground beef, transfer to a food processor and process lightly until fine-textured.

Back-to-School
FALL RECIPES

Fiesta Skillet Dinner

Patricia Wissler
Harrisburg, PA

This quick dish was always a favorite at our house when the kids had basketball games or other activities in the evening.

1 lb. ground turkey or beef
1/2 c. onion, chopped
1-oz. pkg. taco seasoning mix
1-1/2 c. water
14-1/2 oz. can stewed tomatoes

1-1/2 c. zucchini, sliced
1 c. frozen corn
1-1/2 c. instant rice, uncooked
1 c. shredded Cheddar cheese

In a skillet over medium heat, cook turkey or beef with onion until no longer pink; drain. Stir in taco seasoning, water, tomatoes with juice, zucchini and corn; bring to a boil. Stir in rice. Reduce heat to medium-low; cover and simmer for 5 minutes, or until rice is tender and liquid is absorbed. Top with cheese; cover and let stand until cheese is melted. Makes 8 to 10 servings.

Cheeseburger Crescent Pie

Joyce Dreibelbis
Wooster, OH

Who said cheeseburgers need to be hot off the grill? All you need are a few ingredients and 30 minutes to bake this all-American classic. Top with lettuce and tomato after baking, if you like.

1 lb. ground beef
1/2 c. catsup
Optional: 1 T. mustard
1/4 c. dill pickle relish

1- 1/2 c. shredded American or
  Cheddar cheese, divided
8-oz. tube refrigerated
  crescent rolls

Brown beef in a skillet over medium heat; drain. Stir in catsup and mustard, if using. Heat through, stirring occasionally. Stir in relish and one cup cheese. Spoon into an ungreased 9" or 10" glass pie plate. Separate dough into 8 triangles; roll up one-inch on the short side of each triangle. Arrange on top of beef mixture in a spoke pattern, points toward center. Sprinkle with remaining cheese. Bake at 375 degrees for 15 to 20 minutes, until cheese melts. Cut into wedges to serve. Makes 8 servings.

PIZZAS, BURGERS, *Dogs & Tacos*

Quick Chicken Quesadillas

Lisa Adams
Lewistown, PA

This is my go-to meal whenever I don't feel like putting a lot of effort into making supper. Served with corn and/or rice on the side, it is tasty and filling.

2 to 3 chicken breasts, cooked and shredded
8-oz. pkg. shredded Cheddar cheese
1/2 c. onion, diced
2 T. taco seasoning mix, or to taste
10 8-inch flour tortillas
Garnish: ranch salad dressing

Combine chicken, cheese, onion and taco seasoning in a bowl. For each quesadilla, spread 1/4 cup chicken mixture onto half of tortilla; fold tortilla in half. Heat a skillet sprayed with non-stick vegetable spray. Add quesadilla; cook over medium heat for 3 to 4 minutes, until golden. Flip onto other side; cook another 3 to 4 minutes. With a pizza cutter, cut quesadillas into 3 triangles. Serve 4 triangles per person, with ranch dressing for dipping. Serves 6 to 8.

Over dinner, ask your children to tell you about books they're reading at school...return the favor by sharing books you loved as a child. You may find you have some favorites in common!

Back-to-School
FALL RECIPES

Slow-Cooker Pizza Pizza

Emilie Britton
New Bremen, OH

A family favorite for Saturday lunch after working or playing outside. I like to prep all items the night before and toss them into the slow cooker just before heading outdoors.

16-oz. pkg. rigatoni pasta,
  uncooked and divided
1-1/2 lbs. ground beef or
  ground pork Italian sausage
3/4 c. onion, chopped
7-oz. jar sliced mushrooms,
  drained

3-oz. pkg. sliced pepperoni
15-oz. jar pizza sauce
2-1/2 c. shredded mozzarella
  cheese
2-1/2 c. shredded Cheddar
  cheese

Divide uncooked pasta in half; return half of pasta to the pantry for another recipe. In a large skillet over medium heat, brown beef or sausage with onion; drain. In a 6-quart slow cooker, layer half each of beef or sausage mixture, reserved uncooked pasta, mushrooms, pepperoni, pizza sauce and both cheeses. Repeat layers. Cover and cook on low setting for 3 to 4 hours. Check occasionally to make sure pasta is covered with sauce to avoid drying out. Serves 6 to 8.

Keep some festive paper plates and napkins tucked away...
they'll set a lighthearted mood on busy school nights,
plus easy clean-up afterwards.

PIZZAS, BURGERS,
Dogs & Tacos

After-School Pizza

Melody Lenard
Grayson, LA

I can remember growing up in a small rural school district and everyone could hardly wait for "pizza day." Now I make this for my daughter and her friends as an after-school snack. It is very tasty, very easy to make and a hit with all my daughters' friends.

13.4-oz. tube refrigerated
   pizza dough
1 lb. ground beef
1 onion, chopped
1 green pepper, chopped

16-oz. can Sloppy Joe sauce
1 to 2 c. shredded mozzarella
   cheese
Garnish: other favorite pizza
   toppings

Spray a 13"x9" baking pan with non-stick vegetable spray. Unroll pizza dough; press into pan and set aside. In a skillet over medium heat, cook beef with onion and green pepper until beef is browned and vegetables are tender. Drain; stir in Sloppy Joe sauce and heat through. Spoon beef mixture over pizza crust; spread cheese over beef. Add toppings as desired. Bake at 350 degrees for about 15 minutes, until pizza crust is golden and cheese is melted. Let stand several minutes before cutting into squares. Makes 8 servings.

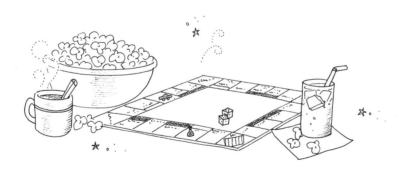

Pizza popcorn...a crunchy snack that's ready in a jiffy! Combine 1/4 cup grated Parmesan cheese, 2 teaspoons each Italian seasoning and paprika, and one teaspoon each onion powder and garlic powder. Sprinkle over a big bowl of buttered popcorn, add salt to taste and toss to mix well.

153

Back-to-School
FALL RECIPES

Chili Chicken Tacos

Beth Flack
Terre Haute, IN

A family favorite...easy to make in your slow cooker. Serve Mexican rice on the side along with chips and salsa or queso.

2 lbs. boneless, skinless chicken breasts
1-1/4 oz. pkg. taco seasoning mix
1 T. brown sugar, packed
4-1/2 oz. can chopped green chiles
1 c. canned corn, drained

10-oz. can enchilada sauce
4 green onions, chopped
4.7-oz. pkg. corn taco shells
Garnish: shredded Mexican-blend cheese, shredded lettuce, chopped tomato, sour cream

Place chicken in a 5-quart slow cooker. Sprinkle with taco seasoning and brown sugar. Add chiles and corn; spoon enchilada sauce over all. Cover and cook on low setting for 6 to 7 hours; add onions during the last 15 minutes of cooking. Shred chicken with 2 forks; stir back into mixture in slow cooker. Meanwhile, bake taco shells according to directions. Serve chicken mixture in taco shells with desired toppings. Makes 6 servings.

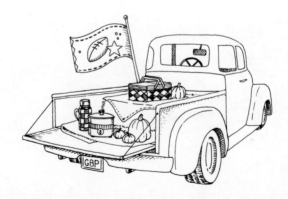

Do you love tailgating, but can't score tickets to the big stadium football game? Tailgating at the local Friday-night high school game can be just as much fun for all ages. Round up the gang, pack a picnic and cheer on your team!

GAME-DAY &
After-School
Snacks

Back-to-School
FALL RECIPES

Devilish Ham & Cheese Log

Lynda Hart
Bluffdale, UT

My neighbor always had this on hand for guests after trick-or-treating. It's a great snack for Halloween.

1 c. shredded sharp Cheddar
  cheese, room temperature
8-oz. pkg. cream cheese, room
  temperature
4-1/2 oz. can deviled ham

1/2 c. chopped black olives,
  drained
1/2 c. chopped pecans
snack crackers or toast points

Beat cheeses in a bowl until well blended. Beat in deviled ham; stir in olives. Cover and chill until almost firm. Shape into 2 logs; roll in pecans. Serve with crackers or toast points. Makes 24 servings.

Host a fun-filled pumpkin party this year! Guests can bring their own pumpkins and cutting tools, while you set out water-based paints, glue sticks, glitter and stickers for the kids to use. Serve up some simple snacks for a memorable occasion.

GAME-DAY & *After-School Snacks*

Guilt-Free Vegetable Dip

Jackie Daunce
Lockport, NY

Mom used to make this simple vegetable dip when I was a kid.
I always thought it was a nice treat! It's a good way to enjoy all the
wonderful veggies in season...extra tasty with green sweet peppers!

8-oz. container fat-free
   cottage cheese
1-1/2 c. light or fat-free
   mayonnaise
1/4 c. onion, finely chopped
1 to 2 T. hot pepper sauce,
   or to taste

1/4 t. garlic powder
1/4 t. salt
1/8 t. pepper
sliced fresh vegetables

In a large bowl, combine cottage cheese and mayonnaise. Beat with an
electric mixer on medium speed for 2 to 4 minutes, until creamy. Stir in
remaining ingredients except vegetables. Spoon into a serving dish;
cover and chill for 30 minutes. Serve with sliced vegetables. Makes
16 servings.

A jug of cider with a mulling spice bag makes a thoughtful
hostess gift. Fill a small muslin drawstring bag with
2 teaspoons each of cloves, allspice and orange zest. Tie it to
a gallon jug of cider along with 4 to 6 cinnamon sticks and a note
that says: "Simmer spices in cider until hot and bubbly...enjoy!"

Back-to-School
FALL RECIPES

Cheesy Corn Dog Bites

Darrell Lawry
Kissimmee, FL

A great little finger food for kids!

8-1/2 oz. pkg. corn muffin mix
10-3/4 oz. can Cheddar cheese
  soup

1 egg, beaten
12 mini cocktail wieners
Garnish: catsup or mustard

Combine muffin mix, soup and egg in a bowl; stir well until batter is
moistened. Fill 12 greased muffin cups with 3 tablespoons batter each;
top each with a wiener. Bake at 400 degrees for 15 minutes, or until
muffins are golden. Cool in pan on a wire rack for 5 minutes before
removing from pan. Garnish as desired. Makes one dozen.

Picante Salsa Dip

Keisha Pittman
Arkadelphia, AR

This is our family's favorite dip...it's delicious on tortilla roll-ups too.
The night before Thanksgiving, we'd always have chips and dips set
out as everyone arrived at my grandmother's house. It's a memory
I will never forget!

2 8-oz. pkgs. cream cheese,
  softened
16-oz. jar medium chipotle salsa

tortilla chips
Optional: flour tortillas

In a bowl, combine cream cheese and salsa. Beat with an electric mixer
on medium speed until mixed. Beat on high speed for 5 to 10 minutes,
until fluffy. For best flavor, cover and chill overnight. Makes 4 cups.

A 250-degree oven keeps hot appetizers
toasty until serving time.

Sausage Queso Dip

Sharon Nunn
Mechanicsville, VA

This is my dad's favorite game-day recipe. He always requests it, and says it's so good it should be illegal! Very easy to make...even easier to enjoy. Choose mild or hot tomatoes to your taste.

1 lb. ground regular or hot
  pork sausage
32-oz. pkg. pasteurized process
  cheese, cubed

10-oz. can diced tomatoes with
  green chiles
tortilla chips or corn chips

Brown sausage in a skillet over medium heat. Drain well; blot with paper towels to absorb excess grease. In a large microwave-safe dish, combine sausage, cheese and undrained tomatoes. Microwave on high for 3 minutes; stir. Continue microwaving for one-minute intervals, stirring each time, until well blended and cheese is melted and smooth. May transfer to a slow cooker set on low to keep warm for serving. Serve with tortilla chips or corn chips. Makes 10 to 12 servings.

Both of my children have always loved carving jack-o'-lanterns for Halloween. The first weekend in October, I take them to a local farm so they can select the perfect pumpkins. A few days before Halloween, we spend an evening laughing together and carving the pumpkins into special designs. Their spooky creations are the perfect touch on our front porch. My son is in college now, but he always checks up to make sure his sister and I are continuing the pumpkin-carving tradition!

– Leslie Harvie, Simpsonville, SC

Back-to-School
FALL RECIPES

Chicken Pinwheels

Caroline Timbs
Cord, AR

These pinwheels are easy to create and hard to resist.
They fill up an appetizer tray in no time!

2 5-oz. cans chicken breast, drained and flaked
8-oz. pkg. cream cheese, softened
1/2 c. shredded Cheddar cheese
1/4 c. grated Parmesan cheese
1/4 c. real bacon bits
2 T. olive oil mayonnaise
1-oz. pkg. ranch salad dressing mix
1 t. pepper
4 to 6 8-inch flour tortillas

In a large bowl, combine all ingredients except tortillas; mix well. Spread a layer of chicken mixture over each tortilla. Roll up; wrap in plastic wrap and chill. At serving time, cut into one-inch slices. Makes 2 dozen.

BLT Roll-Ups

Coleen Lambert
Luxemburg, WI

These are so super easy and tasty! Great for tailgate parties.

8-oz. pkg. cream cheese, softened
1/2 c. mayonnaise
8 to 10 slices bacon, crisply cooked and crumbled
1 c. roma tomatoes, chopped and drained
4 to 6 8-inch flour tortillas
1 c. lettuce, shredded

Blend cream cheese and mayonnaise in a large bowl. Stir in bacon and tomatoes. Spread mixture on tortillas; top with lettuce. Roll up tightly; wrap in plastic wrap and refrigerate for one hour. Slice 1/2-inch thick for serving. Serves 4 to 8.

Tortillas in a variety of flavors like spinach and sun-dried tomato can add variety to a platter of roll-ups.

GAME-DAY &
After-School Snacks

Pepperoni Pinch Me's

Amy Thomason Hunt
Traphill, NC

A super-easy pull-apart bread to serve as a party appetizer or after-school snack. Kids love pinching off pieces to nibble!

6-oz. pkg. sliced pepperoni
1 c. onion, diced
3/4 c. cherry tomatoes, halved
   and drained
1/4 c. zesty Italian salad dressing

1-1/2 c. shredded mozzarella
   cheese
13.4-oz. tube refrigerated pizza
   dough, cut into one-inch
   cubes

In a greased 13"x9" baking pan, combine pepperoni, onion, tomatoes and salad dressing. Sprinkle with cheese; top with dough pieces. Bake, uncovered, at 400 degrees for 30 minutes, or until hot and bubbly. Invert onto serving platter; serve warm. Serves 6.

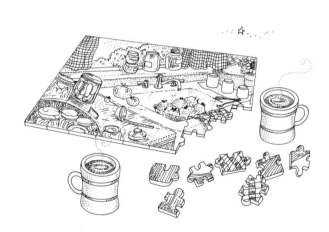

Family night! Serve a simple supper, then spend
the evening playing favorite board games or assembling
jigsaw puzzles together.

Back-to-School
FALL RECIPES

Karen's Crunchy Snack Mix

Karen Gierhart
Fremont, OH

This is a great snack mix to munch on while watching football or your favorite Halloween movies. For a less salty taste, use all garlic and onion powder instead of the garlic and onion salt. Enjoy!

16-oz. pkg. brown sugar oat
   cereal squares
3 c. crunchy cheese corn snacks
2 c. pretzel sticks, broken
1 c. margarine, melted

3/4 c. grated Parmesan cheese
1/2 t. garlic salt
1/4 t. garlic powder
1/2 t. onion salt
1/4 t. onion powder

Combine cereal, corn snacks and pretzels in a large bowl; toss to mix and set aside. In a small bowl, combine melted margarine, cheese and seasonings. Pour margarine mixture over cereal mixture; stir to coat well. Spread evenly on an ungreased 15"x10" jelly-roll pan. Bake at 325 degrees for 20 minutes, stirring occasionally. Let cool; store in a tightly covered container. Makes 12 servings.

Guests will love little bags of snack mix or candied nuts as a take-home gift. Tie on nametags and use them as placecards, or simply heap them in a basket near the front door.

GAME-DAY &
After-School
Snacks

Roasted Pumpkin Seeds, 2 Ways   *Julie Dossantos*
Fort Pierce, FL

I have fond memories of cleaning out our family pumpkin for Halloween with my mother and my sister. We always roasted the seeds with just a little salt. I wanted to experiments with some of my family's favorite spices, and tried something new. This was a hit!

2 to 4 c. fresh pumpkin seeds,
   cleaned
1-1/2 T. olive oil, divided

1 t. curry powder
1 t. lemon pepper seasoning
kosher salt to taste

After cleaning the pumpkin seeds, lay them out on a paper towel-lined baking sheet to dry overnight. To prepare, divide pumpkin seeds between 2 baking sheets; drizzle with olive oil. Season one pan of seeds with curry powder and the other with lemon pepper. Season both pans with salt to taste. Shake and stir seeds with a spatula to distribute oil and seasonings. Bake at 350 degrees for 30 minutes, or until toasty and golden, stirring again after 15 minutes. After 30 minutes, transfer seeds to paper towel-lined baking sheets to drain and cool. Taste and add more seasonings, if desired. Measure out 1/4 cup servings into plastic sandwich bags for a quick, healthy snack. Makes 4 to 6 servings.

New plastic pails make whimsical picnic servers for party chips and snacks. Afterwards, the kids can use them for trick-or-treating.

Back-to-School
FALL RECIPES

Yummy Buckeye Dip

Rebecca Etling
Blairsville, PA

Everyone just loves this recipe...you may want to double it!

1/2 c. creamy peanut butter
1/2 c. cream cheese, softened
2 T. milk
1 c. powdered sugar
8-oz. container frozen whipped
   topping, thawed

12-oz. pkg. mini semi-sweet
   chocolate chips
graham cracker sticks
   or pretzels

In a large bowl, mix together peanut butter, cream cheese and milk until blended. Add powdered sugar; blend well. Fold in whipped topping and chocolate chips. Cover and chill for one hour. Serve with graham cracker sticks or pretzels. Serves 6 to 8.

Autumn Apple Dip

Leslie Harvie
Simpsonville, SC

My kids and I enjoy snacking on this sweet dip while we carve our Halloween pumpkins.

8-oz. pkg. cream cheese,
   softened
3/4 c. brown sugar, packed

1 t. vanilla extract
1 c. chopped peanuts
apple slices

In a bowl, combine all ingredients except apples; mix well. Cover and chill until serving time. Serve with apple slices. Serves 16.

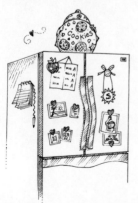

Find a reason to celebrate! Kids will love it when you recognize their achievements like an A in math, a game-winning goal or a new scout badge...in a big way.

GAME-DAY &
After-School
Snacks

Pumpkiny Fluff

Jill Ball
Highland, UT

This is a great easy fall recipe. You can enjoy it as a dip for apple slices, a filling for a frozen pie, or as my children like it, spread between two graham crackers.

15-oz. can pumpkin
1-1/2 oz. pkg. sugar-free instant
    vanilla pudding mix
8-oz. container regular or
    fat-free frozen whipped
    topping, thawed

pumpkin pie spice to taste
sliced apples or graham
    crackers

In a large bowl, combine pumpkin, dry pudding mix, whipped topping and spice in order given; mix well. Cover and refrigerate for 2 hours. Serve with sliced apples or graham crackers. Makes 4 to 6 servings.

As soon as the leaves start to turn, a trip to the local farm is a must for us. Cider doughnuts, apples and a hayride are a treat for everyone. Best of all...picking out a pumpkin. That always takes longer than planned, but finally everyone finds their perfect pick. The only rule is: you have to be able to carry it by yourself to the cash register! Can you picture two determined little boys staggering through the patch, each hugging an enormous pumpkin? What a prize! And what a memory!

– Linda Davis Siess, Amesbury, MA

Back-to-School
FALL RECIPES

Bar-B-Que Meatballs

LaShelle Brown
Mulvane, KS

These meatballs are so delicious with their homemade barbecue sauce. This is definitely a family favorite!

1 to 1-1/2 lbs. ground beef	1/2 c. onion, chopped
1 egg, beaten	1/4 t. garlic powder
3/4 c. rolled oats, uncooked	1/4 t. chili powder

Combine all ingredients in a large bowl. Mix well and roll into one-inch meatballs. Arrange meatballs in a lightly greased 13"x9" baking pan. Spoon Barbecue Sauce evenly over meatballs. Bake, uncovered, at 350 degrees for one hour, or until hot and bubbly. Serves 6.

Barbecue Sauce:

1 c. catsup	4 to 5 t. smoke-flavored
1/2 c. brown sugar, packed	cooking sauce
1/2 c. onion, chopped	1/4 t. salt

Combine all ingredients in a bowl; mix well.

Did you know a prize-winning pumpkin gains about 20 to 30 pounds a day at its peak growing time? That's a lot of pumpkin!

GAME-DAY & *After-School Snacks*

Garden Hummus Dip

Constance Bockstoce
Dallas, GA

This is both kid and grown-up friendly! I wanted to make my own hummus that would be more nutritious and lighter than those on the market. I now double the recipe and eat it more often. Delicious on avocado toast too.

16-oz. can chickpeas, drained
2 carrots, peeled and cut into
  chunks
2 stalks celery with leaves,
  cut into chunks
2 T. olive oil

1 t. onion powder
1 t. garlic powder
pepper to taste
snack crackers, tortilla chips
  or sliced vegetables

In a food processor, combine chickpeas, carrots, celery, oil and seasonings. Process until smooth, about 5 minutes. Transfer to a bowl; cover and refrigerate up to 7 days or freeze. Serve with crackers, tortilla chips or vegetables. Makes 4 servings.

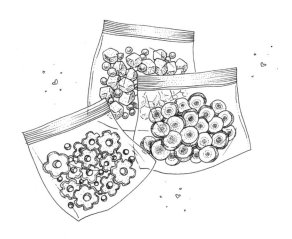

Fresh, colorful veggies are always welcome at parties and are easy to prepare in advance. Cut them into bite-size slices, flowerets or cubes and tuck away in plastic zipping bags until needed...what a time-saver!

Back-to-School
FALL RECIPES

Honey-Glazed Chicken Wings

Jackie Smulski
Lyons, IL

Sweet yet spicy, these appetizer wings are sure to please at tailgating parties and family get-togethers. Be sure to have plenty of napkins on hand!

3 lbs. chicken wings, separated
2 T. olive oil
1 t. kosher salt
1/2 t. pepper

1/2 c. honey
1/4 c. butter
2 cloves garlic, minced
1/2 to 1 t. red pepper flakes

In a large bowl, toss together chicken wings, olive oil, salt and pepper. Arrange wings on parchment paper-lined rimmed baking sheets. Bake at 425 degrees for 25 to 30 minutes, turning once after 15 minutes, until golden and juices run clear. Meanwhile, in a small saucepan, combine remaining ingredients. Bring to a boil over medium heat, stirring occasionally, for 2 minutes or until thickened. Brush wings with honey mixture; bake for another 5 to 6 minutes, or until crisp and golden. Makes about 2 dozen.

Make autumn leaf napkin toppers...an easy craft for kids. Roll out polymer clay in colors like orange, gold, red and brown, then cut out with leaf-shaped mini cookie cutters. Cut a small hole at the top with a drinking straw and bake as package directs. Tie each leaf onto a rolled-up dinner napkin with a strand of jute. Sweet!

GAME-DAY &
After-School Snacks

Witches' Brew

Donna Wilson
Maryville, TN

*We have made this yummy hot beverage for years! I just love
the smell of this brew warming in the slow cooker while
I'm getting ready to go out trick-or-treating with my kids.*

2 c. hot brewed black tea
4 c. apricot nectar
1/3 c. brown sugar, packed

1/2 t. cinnamon
1/2 lemon, sliced
1 t. whole cloves

In a 3-quart slow cooker, combine hot tea, apricot nectar, brown sugar and cinnamon; stir well. Stud the lemon slices with cloves; add to slow cooker. Cover and cook on low setting for 4 hours. Remove lemon slices at serving time; serve in mugs. Makes 10 servings.

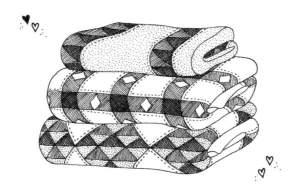

If you're hosting a backyard get-together, toss a few colorful quilts and throws over the chairs. So cozy for snuggling under as the sun sets!

Back-to-School
FALL RECIPES

Crescent Roll Pizza Bites

Leona Krivda
Belle Vernon, PA

These are quick & easy. Sometimes I make them for my grandkids Courtney and Jensen as a snack. They're also great for lunch with a bowl of tomato soup.

8-oz. tube refrigerated crescent
    rolls, separated
48 slices pepperoni
4 pieces mozzarella string
    cheese, each cut in half

1/4 c. butter, melted
garlic powder to taste
Optional: warmed pizza sauce

At the wide end of each crescent roll, place 6 slices of pepperoni; place 1/2 piece of string cheese on top. Roll up, starting at the wide end and tucking in the sides. Place rolls on a lightly greased baking sheet, point-side down. Bake at 375 degrees for 12 to 16 minutes, until golden. Remove from oven; immediately brush lightly with butter and sprinkle lightly with garlic powder. Serve with pizza sauce for dipping, if desired. Serves 4, 2 pieces each.

Here's a quick trick if you're serving up snack mix or popcorn to a crowd. Use coffee filters as disposable bowls...afterwards, just toss 'em away!

GAME-DAY &
After-School Snacks

Speedy Chicken-Salsa Quesadillas

Joyceann Dreibelbis
Wooster, OH

These yummy quesadillas are easy to make. Serve with veggie slices for a quick snack or meal.

1/2 c. salsa
2 T. mayonnaise-type salad
    dressing
1/2 t. chili powder
8 6-inch flour tortillas

3/4 lb. boneless, skinless,
    chicken breast, cooked
    and sliced
1 c. shredded Mexican 4-cheese
    blend

In a bowl, mix salsa, salad dressing and chili powder; spread evenly onto tortillas. Layer half of each tortilla evenly with chicken and cheese. Fold tortillas in half to enclose filling. Spray a skillet with non-stick vegetable spray; heat over medium heat. Add quesadillas, 2 at a time; cook for 4 for 5 minutes on each side, until lightly golden. Cut each quesadilla into 3 wedges to serve. Serves 4, 6 wedges each.

Caramel Apple Cider

Kathy Grashoff
Fort Wayne, IN

Delicious...smells so good warming in the slow cooker, too!

1/2 gal. apple cider
1/3 c. caramel topping
1/2 t. cinnamon

Garnish: whipped cream,
    cinnamon, additional caramel
    topping

Combine cider, caramel topping and cinnamon in a 3-quart slow cooker. Cover and cook on low setting for 3 to 4 hours. Ladle into mugs and dollop with whipped cream; sprinkle with cinnamon and drizzle with topping. Makes 8 servings.

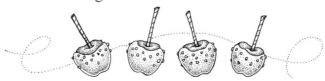

To a young heart, everything is fun.
Charles Dickens

171

Back-to-School
FALL RECIPES

Corn & Bacon Chip Dip

Beth Flack
Terre Haute, IN

This is a favorite dip to enjoy anytime. We serve it for holidays, picnics and tailgating. Good with potato chips and corn chips... I've even served it spooned over baked potatoes!

8-oz. pkg. cream cheese,
   softened
8-oz. container sour cream
1/4 c. mayonnaise
2 cloves garlic, minced

1/2 t. hot pepper sauce
8-oz. can corn, well drained
8 slices bacon, crisply cooked
   and crumbled

In a large bowl, blend cream cheese, sour cream and mayonnaise. Stir in remaining ingredients. Cover and chill 4 hours before serving. Makes 12 servings.

Make your Jack-o'-Lantern creations last longer! Add a tablespoon of bleach to a quart of water, then use a soft cloth to wipe the pumpkin inside & out. Apply a thin layer of petroleum jelly to the cut surfaces.

GAME-DAY &
After-School Snacks

Mild Buffalo Chicken Dip

Teresa Verell
Roanoke, VA

This recipe is a favorite! It is always requested for family get-togethers.

8-oz. pkg. cream cheese, room temperature
1 c. boneless, skinless chicken breast, cooked and chopped
2 T. Buffalo wing sauce

1 c. ranch salad dressing
8-oz. pkg. shredded Colby Jack cheese
tortilla chips, round buttery crackers

Spread cream cheese in an ungreased shallow one-quart casserole dish. Layer with chicken, wing sauce and salad dressing; sprinkle with cheese. Bake, uncovered, at 350 degrees for 20 to 25 minutes, until cheese is melted. Serve warm with tortilla chips and crackers. Makes 10 servings.

I grew up in a neighborhood with lots of kids. To me, it seemed perfect! There were younger kids, the middle group that I was in, and the older group. We would make the biggest piles of leaves and jump into them. For Halloween night, we would get old clothes and stuff them with leaves to make scarecrow bodies, adding heads made out of carved real pumpkins. The scent of fall still makes me smile and sets me right.

— Doreen Knapp, Stanfordville, NY

Back-to-School
FALL RECIPES

Sweet & Salty Pecans

Judy Borecky
Escondido, CA

Once I made 20 pounds of these yummy pecans to help raise money for our grandson's school. There were no pecans left over! You just can't stop eating them. This recipe calls for a lot of black pepper, but trust me, you need this amount.

9 c. pecan halves
1/2 c. agave syrup
1/4 c. pure maple syrup

6 T. sugar
1 T. kosher salt
2 T. pepper

In a large bowl, mix pecans with syrups; stir well and set aside. In a small bowl, mix sugar, salt and pepper; sprinkle over pecans. Stir well to coat pecans. Spread evenly in a 15"x10" jelly-roll pan sprayed with non-stick vegetable spray. Bake at 275 degrees for one hour, stirring after 30 minutes. When done, immediately loosen pecans from pan to avoid sticking. Cool; store in a covered container. Makes 9 cups.

Thanksgiving Snack Mix

Diana Krol
Hutchinson, KS

As a small child, I remember my grandma setting out little bowls of candy corn for all of us cousins at our Thanksgiving family feast. These days, I add some other favorite flavors for the perfect holiday snack mix!

1 c. candy-coated chocolates in
   seasonal colors

1 c. dry-roasted peanuts
1 c. candy corn

In a large bowl, gently stir all ingredients together. Store in a tightly covered container. Makes 3 cups.

The secret to being a relaxed hostess...choose foods that can be prepared in advance. At party time, simply pull from the fridge and serve, or pop into a hot oven as needed.

Harvest Punch

Courtney Stultz
Weir, KS

This easy little beverage was initially going to be called "Witches' Brew" for our Halloween party, but it was so orangey and fun that it was too sweet to be spooky. Great for fun fall parties, Halloween and even Thanksgiving.

1 ltr. lemon-lime soda, chilled
1 ltr. orange soda, chilled
1 ltr. lemon-lime seltzer water,
 chilled

10-oz. jar maraschino cherries,
 drained and juice reserved
ice cubes
Optional: rainbow sherbet

In a punch bowl or pitcher, combine sodas, seltzer, reserved cherry juice and ice as desired. Stir until well blended. Top with a few dollops of sherbet, if desired. Cherries may be added to the punch for serving, or used as a garnish. Makes 10 servings.

For a fruit-studded ice ring that won't dilute your holiday punch, arrange sliced oranges, lemons and limes in a ring mold. Pour in a small amount of punch and freeze until set. Add enough punch to fill mold and freeze until solid. To turn out, dip mold carefully in warm water.

Back-to-School
FALL RECIPES

Hot Tots

Janice Curtis
Yucaipa, CA

Kids of all ages will love this quick appetizer. It's great to go with hot wings on game day or any day!

2 14-1/2 oz. cans queso
  cheese sauce
1 large or 2 small serrano chiles,
  minced and seeds discarded
3/4 c. sour cream

1 c. onion, minced
1/2 c. fresh cilantro, chopped
32-oz. pkg. frozen potato puffs
8-oz. container shredded
  Mexican-blend cheese

In a large bowl, combine all ingredients except potatoes and shredded cheese; mix well. Fold in frozen potato puffs; mix well and transfer to a greased 13"x9" baking pan. Bake, uncovered, at 350 degrees for 45 to 50 minutes, until heated through and potatoes are tender. Top with shredded cheese; return to oven until bubbly and cheese is melted. Serve warm. Serves 8.

Shake up your pumpkin display! Winter squashes come in many sizes, shapes and colors...they're as easy to carve as pumpkins. Speckled green kabocha, bumpy gray Hubbard and ghostly white Lumina all make fun Jack-o'-Lanterns. Heaped uncut in a wooden bowl, they make a fun centerpiece too.

GAME-DAY &
After-School Snacks

Sports-Night Pepperoni Dip

Judy Lange
Imperial, PA

Yummy pepperoni makes this a hit with all ages! It's a great hot snack after a chilly night at the football stadium or ice hockey rink.

4-oz. can chopped black olives, drained
4-oz. jar chopped green olives, drained
1 green pepper, chopped
1 c. Italian salad dressing
8-oz. pkg shredded mozzarella cheese
8-oz. pkg shredded Cheddar cheese
8-oz. pkg pepperoni slices
tortilla chips

In a large bowl, combine olives, green pepper, salad dressing and cheeses. Spread in a lightly greased 13"x9" baking pan; top with pepperoni slices. Bake, uncovered, at 350 degrees for 15 minutes, or until cheese is melted. Serve warm with tortilla chips. Makes 8 servings.

Be sure to have some finger foods for the kids...
tortilla pinwheels, cheese cubes, apple wedges and
mini pigs-in-a-blanket are terrific for little party-goers.

Back-to-School
FALL RECIPES

Parmesan Pretzels

Irene Whatling
West Des Moines, IA

These zesty pretzels are a big hit any time...handy to have on hand for snacking when all those relatives come to visit! They are also good with soup and cheese.

24-oz. pkg. mini twist pretzels
1-1/4 c. oil
1-oz. pkg. ranch salad dressing
  mix

2 T. grated Parmesan cheese
2-1/2 t. Italian seasoning
2 t. garlic powder

Place pretzels in a large paper sack or a large bowl with a lid. Combine remaining ingredients in a separate bowl; mix well and pour over pretzels. Shake sack or bowl until all pretzels are well coated. Spread out pretzels on paper towels to dry; store in an airtight container. Makes 16 servings.

Pizza Snacking Crackers

Barb Bargdill
Gooseberry Patch

Super little snackers...we can't stop nibbling on them!

2 9-oz. pkgs. oyster crackers
1/2 c. canola oil
1/3 c. grated Parmesan cheese

1 T. pizza seasoning blend
1/2 t. garlic powder

Place crackers in a large bowl. In another bowl, combine oil, cheese and seasonings. Pour over crackers; toss gently to coat. Spread evenly on 2 ungreased 15"x10" jelly-roll pans. Bake at 350 degrees for 5 to 7 minutes, stirring once. Cool; store in an airtight container. Makes 8 to 10 servings.

Serve up a Bucket o' Bones at your next Halloween party! Press mini marshmallows onto both ends of pretzel sticks and dip in melted white chocolate.

GAME-DAY &
After-School Snacks

Spicy Snack Crackers

Nadine Rush
London, KY

There's always someone asking me to fix these tasty crackers! My nephews just love them. When I take them to work, everyone takes a handful and passes them around. A very simple and delicious snack to keep on hand.

12-oz. pkg. club crackers
1-1/2 c. canola oil
1 t. cayenne pepper

1.1-oz. pkg. ranch salad
dressing mix

Place crackers in a large bowl with an airtight lid. In a separate bowl, mix oil, cayenne pepper and dressing mix well; pour over crackers. Add lid; turn bowl upside-down and let stand for 30 minutes. Turn bowl right-side up; let stand for 30 more minutes. Continue rotating bowl every 30 minutes for 3 hours. Store crackers in an airtight container. Keeps for weeks and does not get greasy. Serves 12 to 15.

Every Halloween, we get our house ready with flickering lights, decorations and spooky music. We set up a large popcorn machine on the front porch and hand out popcorn instead of candy. We usually have around 400 kids and adults come through in 90 minutes! Lots of fun scary events. We do have help from family & friends, and for our "helpers" we have snacks after the work is done...pizza, hot cider, punch and an assortment of scary cookies, brownies and Scotcharoos. It's a lot of hard work, but its worth it. We all have an awful lot of fun together!
– Debbie Swank, Wauseon, OH

Back-to-School
FALL RECIPES

Best Mexican Dip Ever

Linda McClain
Columbia, NJ

I've been making this recipe for over 25 years, and have been asked to share it many times over...it's enjoyed by all ages!

8-oz. pkg. cream cheese,
   softened
16-oz. can refried beans
15-oz. jar mild, medium or
   hot salsa

8-oz. pkg. shredded Cheddar
   cheese
tortilla chips

Spread cream cheese in a lightly greased 9" deep-dish pie plate or 8"x8" baking pan. Spread beans over cream cheese; spoon salsa over beans and sprinkle shredded cheese evenly on top. Bake, uncovered, at 350 degrees for 20 to 25 minutes, until bubbly and cheese is melted. Serve warm with tortilla chips. Serves 8 to 10.

Brown Sugar Bacon Bites

Linda Belon
Wintersville, OH

Just three ingredients, but oh-so delicious!

1 lb. sliced bacon
14-oz. pkg. mini sausages

3/4 c. brown sugar, packed

Cut each bacon slice into 3 pieces. Wrap each sausage in a piece of bacon; fasten with a wooden toothpick. Arrange sausages on a rimmed baking sheet sprayed with non-stick vegetable spray. Sprinkle with brown sugar. Bake at 375 degrees for one hour. Makes 3 to 4 dozen.

Learn the sweet magic of a cheerful face.
— Oliver Wendell Holmes, Sr.

GAME-DAY &
After-School
Snacks

Cheddar-Sausage
Cornbread Balls

Jasmine Burgess
DeWitt, MI

These are super-simple and easy to toss together. I like to serve these alongside chili or creamy tomato soup...they're perfect for dipping. Sometimes I use Pepper Jack cheese to give them an extra kick.

15-oz. pkg cornbread mix
1 lb. ground pork sausage

3 c. shredded Cheddar cheese
1 c. half-and-half

Add cornbread mix to a large bowl. Break up sausage into small pieces over cornbread mix. Add cheese and toss together with your hands, working cornbread mix into the sausage. Pour half-and-half over all; mix together with your hands. Shape into 2-inch balls; arrange on a parchment paper-lined baking sheet. Bake at 375 degrees for 15 to 20 minutes, until golden. To check for doneness, cut one ball in half. Sausage should be browned, while bread will look moist and solid, yet tender. Makes one to 1-1/2 dozen.

Autumn can be so busy! If time is tight, streamline your holiday plans...just ask your family what traditions and festive foods they cherish the most. Then focus on tried & true activities and free up time to try something new.

Back-to-School
FALL RECIPES

Fresh Tomato Salsa

Bev Traxler
British Columbia, Canada

I make this fresh salsa every September...we love it!
It tastes great with all kinds of chips and works well as
a condiment or added side dish. Fresh is best!

4 c. roma tomatoes, chopped
1/2 c. green pepper, chopped
1 c. white or red onion, diced
1/4 c. fresh cilantro, minced
2 T. fresh lime juice

4 t. jalapeño pepper, chopped
1/2 t. ground cumin
1/2 t. kosher salt
1/2 t. pepper

Combine all ingredients in a large bowl; mix well. Season to taste with more jalapeño, cumin, salt or pepper as desired. Cover and refrigerate. At serving time, stir well; drain some of the excess liquid, if needed. Makes about 5 cups.

"Ghosting" a Halloween buffet? Offer a selection of creepy foods and beverages, labeled with table tents in your spookiest handwriting. If you have a specialty that isn't Halloween-inspired, just give it a spooky new name!

LUNCHBOX
TREATS &
Party Desserts

Back-to-School
FALL RECIPES

Peanut Butter Bars

Janice Schuler
Alburtis, PA

I discovered this recipe 15 years ago and made it for my son's Cub/Boy Scout troop. Every time Matthew went on a camp-out, he took these along. It got to the point that the boys in the scout troop wouldn't even have to ask if he was bringing them...they just assumed he was! At his Eagle Scout Court of Honor, he told them he was "willing the recipe to the troop forever." I am told the troop still insists on having them at the camp-outs. Beware...they won't last long!

1/2 c. butter, melted
3/4 c. creamy peanut butter
1-3/4 c. sugar
1-1/2 t. vanilla extract
4 eggs, lightly beaten

1-1/2 c. all-purpose flour
1/2 t. baking powder
1/4 t. salt
12-oz. pkg. semi-sweet
    chocolate chips

In a large bowl, combine melted butter and peanut butter; stir until thoroughly combined. Stir in sugar and vanilla. Add eggs; stir until blended well. Add flour, baking powder and salt; stir until blended well. Fold in chocolate chips. Spread batter in a greased 13"x9" baking pan. Bake at 350 degrees for 35 minutes, or until golden and a toothpick inserted in the center comes out clean. Cool completely; cut into bars. Makes 2 to 3 dozen.

For bar cookies and brownies, choose a shiny aluminum or gray non-stick coated baking pan. Their surfaces reflect the heat, preventing the bars from baking up too brown and hard.

Mom's Chocolate Snack Cake

Shirley Howie
Foxboro, MA

Mom used to make this simple cake often. We would enjoy a piece of it after school or as a sweet treat after supper, topped with a scoop of vanilla ice cream. I make it now and often keep an extra one in the freezer for a quick & easy dessert.

1 c. boiling water
1/4 c. butter, softened
1 egg, beaten
1 t. vanilla extract
1 c. all-purpose flour
1 c. sugar

3 T. baking cocoa
1 t. baking powder
1/2 t. baking soda
1/4 t. salt
Garnish: powdered sugar

In a large bowl, beat water and butter with an electric mixer on medium-low speed until butter melts. Add egg and vanilla; beat until combined. In a separate bowl, combine remaining ingredients except garnish. Add to egg mixture gradually, beating on low speed until well blended. Pour batter into a greased 8"x8" baking pan. Bake at 350 degrees for 25 to 30 minutes, until a toothpick inserted in the center comes out clean. Cool on a wire rack. Sprinkle with powdered sugar. Makes 9 servings.

Host a neighborhood spruce-up! Everyone can help rake leaves, trim bushes, pull bloomed-out annuals... kids can help too. Afterwards, share cider and doughnuts for a perfect ending to a fun get-together.

Back-to-School
FALL RECIPES

Chocolate Chip Cookie Bars

Pamela Robinson
Saint Paul, VA

Growing up in the 1970s, I never knew that chocolate chip cookies were usually round. Ours were always in cookie bar form, because that's the way my grandmother baked them. Going to her house and enjoying these cookies with her was a major highlight of my life! Grandmother always used walnuts, her favorite nut. I use a variety of nuts and sometimes add butterscotch or peanut butter chips, toffee bits or small candies to change them up. They are always moist and chewy.

2 eggs
1-1/2 c. brown sugar, packed
2/3 c. oil
1 t. vanilla extract

1-1/2 c. self-rising flour
1 c. semi-sweet chocolate chips
Optional: 1/2 c. chopped nuts

In a large bowl, lightly beat eggs. Add brown sugar, oil and vanilla; mix well. Gradually add flour, 1/2 cup at a time. Fold in chocolate chips and nuts, if desired; mix well. Spread batter in an 11"x9" baking pan sprayed with non-stick vegetable spray. Bake at 350 degrees for 25 minutes. Cool completely; cut into large bars. Makes one dozen.

Baking cookies is a terrific activity for first-time cooks. Even the youngest children can help by dropping chocolate chips into the mixing bowl or scooping out spoonfuls of dough. Enjoying the baked cookies together will encourage your little helpers to learn more in the kitchen!

LUNCHBOX TREATS &
Party Desserts

Good Boys Cookies

Lynda Hart
Bluffdale, UT

When my friend's son was young, he would ask his mother to make his favorite cookies and she would tell him, "I'll make them if you'll be a good boy." Soon he began asking her to make the "good boy cookies" and from then on they were called Good Boys. Of course, a good girl may have one, too!

18-1/4 oz. favorite-flavor
   cake mix
1/2 c. oil

2 eggs, beaten
10-1/2 oz. pkg. white or pastel
   mini marshmallows

In a large bowl, combine dry cake mix, oil and eggs; mix thoroughly. Drop dough by teaspoonfuls onto parchment paper-lined baking sheets. Bake at 350 degrees for 6 minutes. Place 5 or 6 mini marshmallows on each cookie; bake 6 minutes longer. Cool completely. If desired, frost with Cream Cheese Icing. Makes 2 dozen.

Cream Cheese Icing:

1/2 c. cream cheese, softened
2 T. butter, softened

4 c. powdered sugar
1 to 2 T. milk

In a large bowl, beat together cream cheese and butter. Beat in powdered sugar until smooth, adding milk to a spreading consistency.

Candy "eyeballs" on Halloween cookies...how much fun is that! Visit the baking department at a grocery or craft store for mini candies and colorful sprinkles to dress up holiday cookies in a jiffy.

Frosted Pumpkin Cookies

Sue Haynes
Scottsdale, AZ

This recipe has been in my family for over 30 years. My grandkids request these cookies and say that they're their favorite!

1 c. sugar	1 t. baking powder
1 c. canned pumpkin	1 t. baking soda
1/2 c. butter, softened	2-1/2 t. cinnamon
2 c. all-purpose flour	1/4 t. salt

In a large bowl, mix together sugar, pumpkin and butter. Stir in remaining ingredients. Drop dough by teaspoonfuls onto ungreased baking sheets. Bake at 375 degrees for 8 to 10 minutes, until lightly golden. Immediately remove cookies to a wire rack; cool. Spread with Light Brown Glaze while glaze is still warm. Makes 2-1/2 dozen.

Light Brown Glaze:

1/4 c. butter	1 t. vanilla extract
2 c. powdered sugar	2 T. milk

Melt butter in a saucepan over medium heat; cook until delicately brown. Stir in powdered sugar and vanilla. Add milk and stir until smooth.

All through my children's school years, I made a tradition of baking each of them their own batch of their favorite kind of cookies to eat when they got home from their first day of school. It was always a treat! I even continued that tradition when they left for college, sending them care packages in the mail. Some things you just cannot let go of!

– Janice Ertola, Martinez, CA

LUNCHBOX TREATS &
Party Desserts

Granny's Fruit Cocktail Cake
Elizabeth Smithson
Mayfield, KY

This recipe came from my granny when I married in 1962. I still keep it handy for whenever I need an easy, fast cake. Wrap squares in wax paper for a perfect lunchbox treat.

2 c. all-purpose flour
1-1/2 c. sugar
1 t. baking soda

1 t. vanilla extract
1 c. chopped pecans
15-oz. can fruit cocktail

Combine all ingredients in a large bowl; do not drain fruit cocktail. Stir until well mixed. Pour batter into a greased 13"x9" baking pan. Bake at 300 degrees for 30 minutes, or until a toothpick inserted in the center tests clean. Pour hot Icing over hot cake; punch holes in cake with a fork and allow icing to soak in. Makes 8 to 10 servings.

Icing:

1/2 c. butter
5-oz. can evaporated milk

1 c. sugar

Melt butter in a saucepan over medium-low heat. Add evaporated milk and sugar. Cook, stirring often, until thickened.

Baking together is a great choice for kids just starting to learn how to cook. As you measure and mix, be sure to share any stories about hand-me-down recipes. You'll be creating memories as well as sweet treats!

189

Back-to-School
FALL RECIPES

Sweet & Salty Crunch Cookies

Courtney Stultz
Weir, KS

Sweet and salty combinations make a great treat, and these cookies are really great! The pretzels, peanuts and chocolate chips give these cookies the perfect sweet & salty taste. I use gluten-free flour and pretzels for this. Great for lunchboxes, gift-giving or enjoying with a cup of hot cocoa or tea!

1/2 c. butter or shortening,
    softened
1/2 c. brown sugar, packed,
    or coconut sugar
1/2 c. honey
1 egg, beaten
1 t. vanilla extract
1-1/4 c. all-purpose flour

1/2 t. baking powder
1/4 t. baking soda
1/2 t. sea salt
1 c. pretzel twists, broken up
1 c. peanuts or other nuts,
    chopped
1/2 c. semi-sweet chocolate chips

In a large bowl, blend together butter, sugar and honey until smooth. Stir in egg and vanilla. Add flour, baking powder, baking soda and salt; mix until just combined. Fold in pretzels, nuts and chocolate chips. Using a cookie scoop or tablespoon, drop dough onto parchment paper-lined baking sheets. Bake at 350 degrees for 10 to 12 minutes, until lightly golden. Remove cookies to a wire rack; cool about 10 minutes. Makes 2 dozen.

A large blackboard makes a great bake sale sign. Pull out lots of colorful chalk to jot down the hours you'll be set up, goodie prices and what your fundraiser is for.

LUNCHBOX TREATS &
Party Desserts

Dressed-Up Popcorn Balls

Paula Marchesi
Auburn, PA

I've been eating this delicious popcorn since I was a little girl and had it at all my birthday parties. Now I make it for all my family and grandchildren for their birthdays too. For a sweeter taste, I add 2 cups shredded coconut to the popcorn. Or you can use 8-1/2 cups popcorn and 2 cups chopped nuts of your choice.

10 c. air-popped popcorn
1/4 c. low-calorie butter or
    butter substitute spread
10-1/2 oz. pkg. mini
    marshmallows

1/4 t. almond extract
1/3 c. white chocolate chips

Place popcorn in a large bowl sprayed with non-stick vegetable spray; set aside. In a saucepan over medium heat, melt butter or butter substitute. Add marshmallows; reduce heat to medium-low. Cook and stir until marshmallows are melted. Remove from heat. Add extract and chocolate chips, stirring until chocolate is melted. Pour marshmallow mixture over popcorn; stir with a wooden spoon until evenly coated. Coat your hands with a little oil; shape mixture into 10 balls. Place balls on a wax paper-lined baking sheet; cool for 15 minutes. Wrap in plastic wrap or cellophane. Makes 10 popcorn balls.

Hurricane globes and thrift store lanterns make wonderful Halloween party lighting...the shabbier, the better! Arrange in a large tabletop or mantel grouping and twine twinkling white lights inside. Battery-operated lights make it kid-friendly.

Back-to-School
FALL RECIPES

Uncle Main's Pumpkin Pie

Martha Buxton
Clio, MI

This recipe is special to me because it came from my uncle, who lives in Florida and is 91 years young. He passed the recipe down, and I've made it my own since the 1970s. I have orders from my family to make it every Thanksgiving and Christmas. My daughter has even requested it for her fall birthday. We all love it!

2 15-oz. cans pumpkin
1/4 c. cornstarch
2/3 c. sweetened condensed milk
4 eggs, beaten
1 T. butter, melted

4 c. sugar
2 T. cinnamon
9-1/2 inch deep-dish pie crust, unbaked
Garnish: whipped cream

In a large bowl, mix pumpkin and cornstarch until smooth. Stir in condensed milk; add eggs and mix well. Add melted butter, sugar and cinnamon; stir well. Pour mixture into pie crust. Bake at 400 degrees for 10 minutes. Reduce oven to 350 degrees; bake for another 45 minutes, or or until a knife tip comes out clean and center of filling is no longer jiggly. Cool; serve with lots of whipped cream. Makes 8 servings.

Warm caramel ice cream topping makes a delightful drizzle over baked apple desserts...pumpkin pie too! Just heat it in the microwave for a few seconds.

LUNCHBOX TREATS &
Party Desserts

Grandma's Pecan Toffee Bars
Kimberly Redeker
Savoy, IL

To me, these are the perfect bars...I love their mix of gooey-ness and cake. I have made this recipe with my grandma since I was a little girl. I still remember the handwritten note card it was on. An easy recipe to make with kids, and enjoyed by all. Thank you, Grandma!

18-1/4 oz. yellow cake mix
2 eggs, divided
1/4 c. butter, melted and
   cooled slightly
14-oz. can sweetened
   condensed milk

1 t. vanilla extract
10-oz. pkg. toffee baking chips
1 c. chopped pecans

Combine dry cake mix, one egg and butter in a bowl. Beat with an electric mixer on medium speed until blended. Spread batter in a greased 13"x9" baking pan. In a separate bowl, beat condensed milk, remaining egg and vanilla until blended. Fold in toffee chips and pecans; spread over batter. Bake at 350 degrees for 25 to 30 minutes; until edges are lightly golden. Topping will not be completely set. Cool completely; cut into 2-inch squares. Makes 2 dozen.

Caramel Apple Cupcakes
Tammy Leber
Gilford, NH

I made these cupcakes when my youngest son wanted to bring a special treat for Halloween to his classmates. Everyone loved them!

18-1/4 oz. pkg. spice cake mix
2 McIntosh apples, peeled, cored
   and diced
14-oz. pkg. caramels, unwrapped

3 T. milk
Optional: chopped walnuts or
   pecans

Prepare cake mix as package directs; fold apples into batter. Spoon batter into 24 greased or paper-lined muffin cups, filling 2/3 full. Bake at 350 degrees for 20 to 25 minutes. Cool cupcakes on a wire rack. Combine caramels and milk in a saucepan over medium heat. Cook, stirring constantly, until completely melted; spread over cupcakes. Sprinkle with nuts, if desired. Makes 2 dozen.

Back-to-School
FALL RECIPES

Popcorn Cake

Melissa Currie
Phoenix, AZ

When I taught third grade, my students would enjoy helping make this fun popcorn cake in the morning, to enjoy in the afternoon before the bell rang to go home. Get ready for ooohs and aahs!

1/2 c. plus 2 T. butter, divided
16-oz. pkg. plain candy-coated
   chocolates, divided
6 c. lightly salted popcorn

16-oz. pkg. peanut candy-coated
   chocolates
16-oz. jar dry-roasted peanuts
16-oz. pkg. marshmallows

Use 2 tablespoons butter to coat a smooth tube pan. Sprinkle a handful of plain candies in bottom of pan and set aside. In a very large bowl, combine popcorn, remaining plain candies, peanut candies and peanuts. In a saucepan over medium heat, melt remaining butter and marshmallows. Stir until smooth; pour over popcorn mixture and mix well. Pack mixture tightly into tube pan; cover and refrigerate at least 1-1/2 hours. Run a knife around edge and center of pan. Invert onto a plate; slice like a cake. Makes 8 to 10 servings.

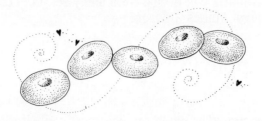

Fall has always been my favorite season. From the brightly colored leaves to the fresh smell in the air, I love it all! What I love most of all is family time. Each fall, my husband and I wake up our three children early to go to a nearby doughnut shop. We watch the doughnuts being made and look forward to eating them. One fall day that I recall, there was the first chill in the air. Grandma & Grandpa came to visit for the day. After a nice lunch at home together, we all walked together to the park, enjoying the spectacular fall weather. There was no place I'd rather be! I live for memories like these.

– Laura Edlund, Papillion, NE

Party Desserts

Candy Corn Cupcakes

Vickie
Gooseberry Patch

Tinted inside like candy corn, these cupcakes are fun for children's parties. I love to add some candy sprinkles! If you don't have orange food coloring, mix 2 drops of yellow coloring to one drop of red.

18-1/4 oz. pkg. white cake mix
1 c. sour cream
orange and yellow food
   coloring gel

Garnish: white frosting,
   candy corn

Prepare cake mix according to package directions; stir sour cream into batter. Divide batter evenly into 2 separate bowls. Color half of batter with a few drops of orange food coloring. Color the other half with a few drops of yellow food coloring. Spoon 1/4 cup yellow batter into 24 paper-lined muffin cups; top with orange batter, filling half full. Bake at 350 degrees for 25 to 30 minutes, until a toothpick tests done. Cool completely on a wire rack. Top cupcakes with a dollop of frosting and a piece of candy corn. Makes 2 dozen.

Doughnut kabobs...what a fun idea for a party!
Slide bite-size doughnuts onto wooden skewers and
stand the skewers in a tall vase for easy serving.

Back-to-School
FALL RECIPES

Fresh Pear Cake

Louise Bowker
Charlotte, TN

I harvest fresh pears in the fall and put them in the freezer, so we can enjoy this cake all winter. It really is a crowd-pleaser.

3 c. pears, cored and diced
2 c. plus 1 T. sugar, divided
3 eggs, beaten
1-1/4 c. canola oil
3 c. all-purpose flour

1 t. baking soda
1 t. salt
2 t. vanilla extract
Optional: 1-1/2 c. chopped
    pecans

In a bowl, sprinkle pears with one tablespoon sugar; mix gently and set aside. In another bowl, beat eggs, oil and remaining sugar with an electric mixer on medium speed until blended. Combine flour, baking soda and salt in another bowl. Add to egg mixture; beat on low speed until blended. Fold in vanilla, pears and pecans, if using. Pour batter into a greased Bundt® pan. Bake at 350 degrees for one hour, or until a toothpick comes out clean. Let cool in pan on a wire rack for 15 minutes; turn out cake onto a plate to cool. Spoon Caramel Frosting over cooled cake; allow to drizzle down sides of cake. Makes 20 servings.

Easy Caramel Frosting:

1/2 c. butter
3 T. milk

1/2 c. brown sugar, packed
1 to 1-1/4 c. powdered sugar

Melt butter in a saucepan over medium heat; add milk and brown sugar. Bring to a boil; cook over low heat for 2 minutes. Beat in powdered sugar to desired consistency.

Juicy fresh pears are one of fall's delights. Green Anjou pears and sandy-colored Bosc will hold their shape nicely when cooked, while red or yellow Bartlett pears are delicious for eating out of hand.

196

LUNCHBOX TREATS &
Party Desserts

Cranberry-Pear-Apple Crisp
Joyceann Dreibelbis
Wooster, OH

This warm dessert with its crunchy topping is filled with all my favorite fall fruits. Perfect for Thanksgiving and for other autumn get-togethers!

8 pears, peeled, cored and sliced
4 apples, peeled, cored and sliced
2 c. fresh cranberries, thawed
   if frozen
1 c. sugar
1-1/2 c. all-purpose flour,
   divided

1 c. brown sugar, packed
3/4 c. quick-cooking oats,
   uncooked
1/2 t. cinnamon
1/2 c. butter

In a large bowl, toss together pears, apples, cranberries, sugar and 3/4 cup flour. Spread mixture in a greased 13"x9" baking pan; set aside. In another bowl, combine remaining flour, brown sugar, oats and cinnamon. Cut in butter with a fork until mixture resembles coarse crumbs; sprinkle over top. Bake, uncovered, at 350 degrees for 60 to 65 minutes, until fruit is tender and topping is golden. Serves 10 to 12.

Treat yourself to a colorful new set of oven mitts and potholders. With all of the baking occasions that autumn and Christmas bring, you will be glad every time you use them!

197

Back-to-School FALL RECIPES

Apple Slab Pie

Lisa Johnson
Hallsville, TX

A family favorite! I found this recipe in one of Mama's recipe books. She had it written on a note card and was using it as a bookmark. So, I'm not sure where it came from...but I'm happy to have it!

14-oz. pkg. refrigerated
  pie crusts
1 c. sugar
3 T. all-purpose flour
1 t. cinnamon
1/4 t. nutmeg
1/4 t. salt

1-1/2 T. lemon juice
9 to 10 Granny Smith, Jonathan
  and/or McIntosh apples,
  peeled, cored and thinly
  sliced
1 c. powdered sugar
2 T. milk

Soften pie crusts as directed on package; remove crusts from package. On a lightly floured surface, unroll and stack crusts, one on top of the other. Roll out into a 21-inch by 17-inch rectangle. Fit combined crust into an ungreased 15"x10" jelly-roll pan, pressing crust into corners. Fold extra crust under, even with the edge of the pan. Crimp edges and set aside. In a large bowl, mix together sugar, flour, spices, salt and lemon juice. Add apples; toss to coat well. Spoon apple mixture into crust-lined pan. Bake at 450 degrees for 33 to 38 minutes, until crust is golden and apples are tender and bubbly. Cool in pan on a wire rack for 30 to 45 minutes. For icing, mix powdered sugar and milk until well blended. Drizzle over pie; allow it to set 30 minutes before serving. Serves 15.

Need a dessert for a tailgating crowd? Bake up a jelly-roll pan recipe like Apple Slab Pie or chocolate sheet cake. These recipes make plenty of servings and are a snap to serve and clean up. They're sure to please everyone too!

LUNCHBOX TREATS &
Party Desserts

Hayride Bundt Cake

Judy Lange
Imperial, PA

*Fall is always a busy time, and hayrides and pumpkin patches
are always a must! Coming home from a day at the farm,
this cake is a great treat for all to enjoy.*

18-1/2 oz. yellow cake mix
3.4-oz. pkg. instant butterscotch
  pudding mix
3 eggs, beaten
1/4 c. water

1/4 c. oil
1 c. canned pumpkin
2 t. pumpkin pie spice
Garnish: whipped cream, vanilla
  or pumpkin ice cream

In a large bowl, combine dry mixes and remaining ingredients except
garnish. Beat with an electric mixer on low speed for 2 minutes. Pour
batter into a greased Bundt® pan. Bake at 350 degrees for 45 to
55 minutes. Cool; turn cake out of pan. Garnish slices of cake as
desired. Serves 10.

At the next school get-together, enjoy the fun of an old-fashioned
pie or cake auction! Bidding on sweet treats made by the
youth group (or by agreeable parents) is a terrific fundraiser
for school activities.

Back-to-School
FALL RECIPES

Confetti Butterscotch Bars

Liz Plotnick-Snay
Gooseberry Patch

These yummy bars are a wonderful way to use candy left over from Halloween. If I don't have enough, sometimes I'll add jumbo candy sprinkles. They add color and fun!

1 c. brown sugar, packed
1 c. plus 2 T. butter, softened
  and divided
1-1/2 t. vanilla extract
1 egg, beaten
2 c. all-purpose flour

1/2 c. light corn syrup
1 c. butterscotch chips
1-1/2 c. assorted candies like
  candy corn and candy-coated
  chocolates
1/2 c. salted peanuts

In a large bowl, combine brown sugar, one cup butter, vanilla and egg. Beat with an electric mixer on medium speed until well blended. Stir in flour. Press dough evenly into an ungreased 13"x9" baking pan. Bake at 350 degrees for 20 to 22 minutes, until lightly golden. Cool for 20 minutes. Meanwhile, in a saucepan over medium heat, cook corn syrup and remaining butter, stirring occasionally, until mixture boils. Add butterscotch chips; stir until melted. Immediately spread butterscotch mixture over baked layer. Sprinkle with candies and peanuts; gently press into butterscotch mixture. Cool for 2 hours, or until butterscotch mixture is firm; do not refrigerate. Cut into bars. Makes about 2-1/2 dozen.

Wrapping up cupcakes for lunchboxes? Split them in half, frost the cut sides and reassemble...wrap and go with no sticky mess! Works great with muffins and cream cheese too.

LUNCHBOX TREATS &
Party Desserts

Indoor S'mores

Julie Warren
Valdosta, GA

My daughter loves s'mores, but we live inside the city limits and can't have a bonfire. This is a great alternative!

3.9-oz. pkg. instant chocolate
   pudding mix
2 c. cold milk
1 sleeve honey graham crackers,
   finely crushed

2 T. butter, melted
1 c. mini marshmallows

In a large bowl, whisk together pudding mix and milk for 2 minutes; set aside. In another bowl, mix crushed graham crackers with melted butter. Put 2 heaping tablespoonfuls of cracker mixture into each of 4 to 5 heat-proof small dessert bowls. Add 2 to 3 heaping tablespoonfuls pudding to each bowl. Sprinkle some of remaining cracker mixture over pudding. Refrigerate until pudding is set. Top each bowl with several mini marshmallows. Place under oven broiler for a few seconds, until marshmallows start to turn lightly golden. Watch closely as this happens quickly. Serves 4 to 5.

Caramel Apples

Jill Valentine
Jackson, TN

These are such fun at Halloween. We like to cover them in mini candy-coated chocolates, candy sprinkles or chopped nuts...yum!

4 to 6 wooden treat sticks
4 to 6 Gala or Jonagold apples
14-oz. pkg. caramels, unwrapped

2 T. milk
Optional: candy sprinkles

Insert treat sticks into apples; set aside. Combine caramels and milk in a microwave-safe bowl. Microwave, uncovered, for 2 minutes, stirring once. Cool briefly. Quickly roll each apple in caramel, turning to coat. Set apples on lightly greased wax paper. When partially set, roll in sprinkles, if desired. Makes 4 to 6 apples.

Back-to-School
FALL RECIPES

Sour Cream Cookies

Nancy Kaiser
York, SC

This was my husband's grandmother's recipe. My father-in-law said that whenever he and his brothers came in from school or from doing their farm chores, his mother always had a jar full of these big, thick, soft and delicious cookies waiting for them. I've revised it somewhat and added the amounts of a few ingredients. I like to use a scalloped round cookie cutter.

1 c. butter-flavored or regular
   shortening
8-oz. container sour cream
2-1/2 c. brown sugar, packed

1 egg, beaten
5-1/2 c. all-purpose flour
1 t. baking soda
1 t. nutmeg

In a large bowl, blend together shortening, sour cream, brown sugar and egg; set aside. In a separate bowl, combine flour, baking soda and nutmeg; mix well and add to shortening mixture. Mix until well blended. Cover and chill for 2 hours, or overnight. On a floured surface, roll out dough about 1/2-inch thick. Cut out with a 3" round cookie cutter; arrange cookies on ungreased baking sheets. Bake at 375 degrees for 13 to 14 minutes. Makes 2-1/2 dozen.

Think what a better world it would be if we all,
the whole world, had cookies and milk about
three o'clock every afternoon and then
lay down on our blankets for a nap.

– Robert Fulghum

LUNCHBOX TREATS &
Party Desserts

Apple Butter Cookies

Deanne Corona
Hampton, GA

Every September, I like to go to the mountains to get Winesap apples. I love to make apple butter with them. It makes my kitchen smell really nice and apple-y. I make so much apple butter that I decided to do something else with my apple butter...I bake cookies. They freeze really nicely.

1/2 c. shortening	1/2 t. salt
1 c. brown sugar, packed	1/2 c. buttermilk
1 egg, beaten	1/2 c. apple butter
3 c. all-purpose flour	Optional: sugar
1/2 t. baking soda	

Add shortening to a large bowl; work shortening with the back of a spoon until fluffy and creamy. Gradually add brown sugar; mix until light. Stir in egg. In another bowl, sift together flour, baking soda and salt. Add flour mixture to shortening mixture alternately with buttermilk; mix well. Cover and chill until dough is easy to handle. Turn out dough onto a lightly floured surface. Roll out 1/8-inch thick. Cut out cookies with a 2-1/2" round cookie cutter. Sandwich cookies together in pairs, with one teaspoon apple butter in between. Press edges together with a fork. Sprinkle with sugar, if desired. Place cookies on greased baking sheets, one inch apart. Bake at 400 degrees for 12 to 15 minutes. Makes 2 dozen.

Fall is a perfect time of year to share some tasty treats with teachers, librarians and school bus drivers...let them know how much they're appreciated!

Back-to-School
FALL RECIPES

Daddy's Pumpkin Custard

Bethi Hendrickson
Danville, PA

What do you do with a fresh pumpkin? At our house, we make dessert! This is a wonderful custard, or add a crust to the pie plate for a fantastic pie. This can be made with either regular sugar or sugar substitute for loved ones (like Daddy) on a low-sugar diet.

1 pie pumpkin, halved and
   seeds removed
2 eggs, beaten
1-1/4 c. evaporated milk, divided
1 t. cornstarch

1/2 c. sugar or 3 envs. sugar
   substitute
1 t. pumpkin pie spice
Garnish: cinnamon or pumpkin
   pie spice, whipped topping

Place pumpkin halves cut-side down on a parchment paper-lined rimmed baking sheet. Bake at 350 degrees for 30 to 40 minutes, until fork-tender. Scoop out pumpkin into a mini mesh colander; drain and cool. Transfer 2 cups pumpkin to a large bowl. Add eggs; mix well and set aside. In a small bowl, combine 1/4 cup evaporated milk and cornstarch. Mix until smooth and add to pumpkin mixture. Add remaining milk, sugar or sweetener and spice; mix until smooth. Pour into a 9" pie plate; sprinkle with spice as desired. Bake at 350 degrees for 40 to 45 minutes. Cool; slice and serve with whipped topping. Serves 8.

Pie pumpkins can serve as Halloween table decorations, then be turned into pies for Thanksgiving. After Halloween, store them in a cool, dry place like a garage, off the floor, with plenty of air circulating around them...ready to bake into delicious pies!

LUNCHBOX TREATS &
Party Desserts

Mother's Baked Apples

Linda Deal
Meyersdale, PA

This recipe has been handed down through generations. My mother made these apples often and now my grandchildren look forward to having them on special occasions. Firm pears may also be used.

6 Yellow Delicious apples, peeled,   1 T. cornstarch
   halved and cored   1 t. cinnamon
3 T. sugar   3/4 c. water
3 T. brown sugar, packed

Place apple halves in a greased 13"x9" baking pan. In a bowl, mix together sugars, cornstarch and cinnamon; add water and stir well. Pour sugar mixture over apples. Bake, uncovered, at 350 degrees for 45 minutes, or until bubbly and apples are tender. Serves 6.

The baker of our family was my German grandmother, who lived next door to us. Everything she made was from scratch...no box mixes for Gram! In the fall, apple pies, apple cakes and apple-walnut strudel were prevalent, along with her ever-present homemade bread. I had the best toast with jam any time of the day! Grandmother didn't have her recipes written down. I used to ask her how I was going to be able to bake like her if I didn't have a recipe? She'd tell me, "Well, it's just a pinch of this and a pinch of that." I sure miss my Gram!

– Norma Murphy, Orinda, CA

Back-to-School
FALL RECIPES

Peanut Butter & Jam Bars

Sandra Mirando
Depew, NY

After I made a pan of these delicious bars and sampled one,
I knew the recipe had to be shared. You will love them! Be sure
to use raspberry jam, not jelly.

1 c. butter, room temperature
1-1/2 c. sugar
1 t. vanilla extract
2 eggs, beaten
16-oz. jar crunchy peanut butter
3 c. all-purpose flour

1 t. baking powder
1-1/2 t. kosher salt
18-oz. jar raspberry jam
2/3 c. salted peanuts, coarsely
   chopped

In a large bowl, beat butter and sugar with an electric mixer on medium speed for about 2 minutes, until light yellow. Turn mixer to low speed. Add vanilla, eggs and peanut butter; beat until well combined. Add flour, baking powder and salt; beat just until well combined. Dough will be thick. Spread 2/3 of dough in a greased and floured 13"x9" baking pan. Spread jam over dough. Break remaining dough into small pieces and scatter over jam. Sprinkle with peanuts. Bake at 350 degrees for 45 minutes, or until golden. Cool; cut into squares. Makes 2 dozen.

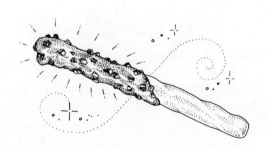

A sweet & salty treat in a jiffy! Simply dip pretzel rods in melted chocolate. Drizzle with white chocolate or candy melts in seasonal colors and roll in candy sprinkles. For party favors, wrap individually in plastic wrap and tie with a bow.

LUNCHBOX TREATS &
Party Desserts

Fruit Empanadas

Gayla Reyes
Fairfield, OH

*We like strawberry preserves in these cookies! They're rolled
twice in powdered sugar for extra sweetness.*

1 c. butter, softened
3/4 c. cream cheese, softened
2 c. all-purpose flour

32-oz. jar favorite fruit preserves
1 to 2 c. powdered sugar

In a large bowl, blend butter and cream cheese until smooth. Beat in
flour; shape dough into a ball. Wrap in plastic wrap; refrigerate
overnight, or up to one week. Let dough stand at room temperature for
30 minutes. On a floured surface, roll out chilled dough thinly. Cut out
cookies with a 3" round cookie cutter. Add 1-1/2 teaspoons preserves
to the center of each cookie. Moisten edges; fold in half and press edges
together, to form a crescent shape. Place on ungreased baking sheets.
Bake at 375 degrees for 15 to 20 minutes. Immediately roll cookies in
powdered sugar. Cool; roll again in powdered sugar. Makes 2 dozen.

Cranberry Crunch Delight

Lisa Barger
Conroe, TX

*This recipe came from a very old pamphlet from years ago. It is
as good today as it was back then! This dish can be halved
beautifully in an 8"x8" pan.*

2 c. rolled oats, uncooked
1 c. all-purpose flour
2 c. brown sugar, packed

1 c. butter, softened
2 15-oz. cans whole-berry
   cranberry sauce

In a large bowl, combine oats, flour and brown sugar; mix thoroughly.
Add butter; blend until evenly combined and crumbly. Spread half of
crumb mixture in a greased 13"x9" baking pan; press down. Spread
cranberry sauce evenly over oat mixture; sprinkle remaining crumb
mixture over cranberries. Bake at 350 degrees for 40 minutes, or until
until crumb topping is lightly golden. Makes 8 to 10 servings.

Back-to-School
FALL RECIPES

Homemade Doughnuts

Carol Kemnitz
Palmdale, CA

Whenever our children were doing well in school and piano practice was accomplished, we celebrated on Friday nights with homemade doughnuts. They're perfect with a mug of cider or milk...yum!

4 c. all-purpose flour	1/4 c. butter, melted
1 c. sugar	1/4 t. cinnamon
2 eggs, beaten	1/4 t. nutmeg
1 c. milk	1/4 t. ground mace
4 t. baking powder	canola oil for deep-frying

In a large bowl, combine all ingredients except oil. Cover and chill for 5 minutes. On a floured surface, roll out dough 1/2-inch thick. Cut out doughnuts with a doughnut cutter. In a deep saucepan over medium-high heat, bring 2 inches oil to 370 degrees. Working in batches, drop in 2 to 3 doughnuts; cook until golden and doughnuts float to the top. Turn over and cook other side until golden. (Doughnut holes will cook in about 30 seconds.) With a slotted spoon, remove doughnuts to paper towels; drain. Makes one to 1-1/4 dozen.

Whip up a tasty apple cider glaze for doughnuts. Mix up 2-1/2 cups powdered sugar and 1-1/2 teaspoons apple pie spice. Stir in 1/4 cup apple cider until a drizzling consistency is reached.

LUNCHBOX TREATS &
Party Desserts

Chocolate-Peanut Butter Haystacks

Hannah Thiry
Luxemburg, WI

These crunchy and delicious no-bake cookies just take a few minutes!
Even older kids can make them, as easy as 1-2-3.

1-1/2 c. semi-sweet
  chocolate chips
1-1/2 c. peanut butter chips

1 c. salted peanuts
2 to 2-1/2 c. chow mein noodles

In a large saucepan over medium-low heat, combine chocolate and peanut butter chips. Cook and stir until melted. Add peanuts and noodles; stir until well coated. Drop mixture by tablespoonfuls onto wax paper-lined baking sheets. Let stand for several hours, until set. Makes 2 dozen.

Oops! Your child just reminded you that she's bringing the class treats tomorrow. Whip up cake-mix cookies quickly...great with any flavor of cake mix! Mix together an 18-ounce box of cake mix, 2 eggs, 2 tablespoons melted shortening and 1/4 cup water. Drop by teaspoonfuls onto a greased baking sheet and bake at 350 degrees for 10 minutes. Presto, cookies!

Back-to-School
FALL RECIPES

Peanut Butter Balls

Gretchen Brown
Hillsboro, OR

I have made these little treats every year for twenty years...my husband and kids always so look forward to them. Once, I tried to get away without making them and there was quite an uproar by family & friends! They are so good.

1-1/2 c. crispy rice cereal	2 c. creamy peanut butter
2-1/4 c. powdered sugar	2 c. milk chocolate chips or
1/4 c. butter	melting chocolate

Combine cereal and powdered sugar in a large bowl; mix well and set aside. In a saucepan over medium-low heat, melt together butter and peanut butter; pour over cereal mixture. Mix with your hands; form into balls. Place on wax paper-lined baking sheets. Chill for one hour. Melt chocolate according to package directions; dip balls in chocolate. Return to baking sheets; chill until chocolate sets. Makes 4 dozen.

Chocolate Marshmallow Fudge

Wendy Jo Minotte
Duluth, MN

This fudge makes great gifts without too much work. Share with your friends and enjoy!

2 T. butter, softened and divided	1 t. vanilla extract
12-oz. can evaporated milk	4-1/2 c. mini marshmallows
5 c. sugar	2 12-oz. pkgs. milk chocolate
1 t. salt	chips

Use one tablespoon butter to coat a 17"x11" jelly-roll pan or two, 13"x9" baking pans; set aside. In a large heavy saucepan, combine remaining butter, evaporated milk, sugar and salt. Bring to a boil over medium heat. Boil for 10 minutes, stirring constantly. Remove from heat. Stir in remaining ingredients, stirring vigorously until marshmallows and chocolate chips are completely melted. Pour into pan(s). Cool completely; cut into one-inch squares. Makes about 8 dozen.

LUNCHBOX TREATS &
Party Desserts

Quick & Easy Halloween Bark
Stephanie Turner
Meridian, ID

Need a quick last-minute treat for a Halloween party?
This recipe is great for kids to help prepare. Only four ingredients
and prep time is about five minutes!

1 lb. white melting chocolate
15 chocolate and orange
  sandwich cookies, broken up
  into large chunks
1 c. candy corn

1 c. thin pretzel sticks, broken
  into one-inch pieces
Optional: seasonal candy
  sprinkles

Line a 17"x11" or 15"x10" jelly-roll pan with wax paper; set aside.
In a microwave-safe dish, melt chocolate on high in 20 to 30-second
intervals, stirring in between, until smooth and shiny. Pour chocolate
onto pan; spread evenly with a spatula. Quickly arrange remaining
ingredients over melted chocolate. With a piece of wax paper, gently
press toppings into chocolate. Refrigerate for 30 minutes, or until set
and firm. Break into pieces. Serves 20.

Chocolate Poodles
Lisa Barger
Conroe, TX

Such a funny name for cookies! This recipe is from an old cookbook
of mine...you may know them as no-bake cookies. Enjoy!

2 c. sugar
1/2 c. butter
1/2 c. milk
1/4 c. baking cocoa

1 t. vanilla extract
3 c. quick-cooking oats,
  uncooked

In a saucepan over medium heat, combine sugar, butter, milk and
cocoa. Bring to a boil; cook for 1-1/2 minutes. Remove from heat. Add
vanilla and oats; stir until well combined. Drop onto wax paper-lined
baking sheets by tablespoonfuls. Refrigerate until set and firm. Makes
about 3 dozen.

Back-to-School
FALL RECIPES

Sugar Cookies Extraordinaire

Donna Carter
Ontario, Canada

A good friend of mine gave me this recipe many years ago. Over the years, I have revamped it to make it my own. Can be made any time of year and oh-so delicious! The secret is in the vinegar.

1 c. margarine, softened	1 t. baking soda
3/4 c. plus 1/2 c. sugar, divided	2 t. vinegar
1-3/4 c. all-purpose flour	1 t. vanilla extract

In a large bowl, blend together margarine and 3/4 cup sugar. Add flour and baking soda; mix well. Add vinegar and vanilla; stir until consistency is even. Roll dough into golf-ball size balls; roll in remaining sugar. Arrange 2 inches apart on parchment paper-lined baking sheets. Bake at 350 degrees for 12 to 15 minutes. Cool completely on a wire rack before serving. Makes about 2 dozen.

As I think of this beautiful autumn day, I'm already in the mood to bake a cherry or apple pie for my neighbor and me. He shares his garden vegetables with the neighborhood, so I return the favor with treats throughout the seasons for him. My passion is not television nor computers. I love paging through my dozens of cookbooks, and finding new recipes to try.

— Alice Happe, Sikeston, MO

LUNCHBOX TREATS &
Party Desserts

Special Oatmeal Cookies

Karen Antonides
Gahanna, OH

Whenever I went back to South Dakota to visit my mom, her friend Elvina would stop over with these special cookies. They were great to eat while visiting with friends from back home. The addition of coconut makes these cookies so flavorful!.

1/2 c. butter, softened	1 t. baking powder
1/2 c. sugar	1 t. baking soda
1/2 c. brown sugar, packed	1/2 t. salt
1 egg, beaten	1 c. quick or old-fashioned oats,
1/2 t. vanilla extract	uncooked
1-1/4 c. all-purpose flour	1 c. flaked coconut

In a large bowl, combine butter, sugars, egg and vanilla; mix well. Add flour, baking powder, baking soda and salt; mix well. Stir in oats and coconut. Cover and refrigerate dough for several hours or overnight. Shape dough into one-inch balls; place on greased baking sheets. Bake at 350 degrees for 12 to 15 minutes. Makes 3 dozen.

Snickerdoodles

Judy Taylor
Butler, MO

Many years ago, a friend made these cookies for my family when I was ill. No other snickerdoodle cookies compare to this great recipe.

1 c. shortening	2 t. cream of tartar
2 c. sugar, divided	1 t. baking soda
2 eggs, beaten	1/2 t. salt
2-3/4 c. all-purpose flour	2 T. cinnamon

In a bowl, blend shortening and 1-1/2 cups sugar; stir in eggs. Add remaining ingredients except cinnamon; mix well. Form dough into walnut-size balls. Combine cinnamon and remaining sugar; coat balls in cinnamon-sugar. Place on greased baking sheets. Bake at 375 degrees for 10 minutes, or until cookies start to look cracked on the top. Do not overbake. Place baking sheet on a wire rack; cool. Makes 2 to 2-1/2 dozen.

Back-to-School
FALL RECIPES

Glazed Cinnamon Apples

Marcia Marcoux
Charlton, MA

This is a delicious, warm slow-cooker dessert. How great it is to walk into the house after raking leaves and smell the cinnamon and apples, ready for a treat!

6 Granny Smith apples, peeled, cored and cut into 8 wedges
1 T. lemon juice
1/2 c. sugar
1/2 c. light brown sugar, packed
2 T. all-purpose flour

1 t. cinnamon
1/4 t. nutmeg
6 T. butter, melted
Garnish: vanilla ice cream
Optional: crumbled oatmeal or gingersnap cookies

Add apples to a 5-quart slow cooker; drizzle with lemon juice. Mix sugars, flour and spices in a bowl. Sprinkle over apples; stir gently to coat apples. Drizzle with butter. Cover and cook on low setting for 3 hours, or on high setting for 2 hours, until apples are tender. To serve, spoon warm apple mixture over ice cream; sprinkle with crumbled cookies, if desired. Serves 6 to 8.

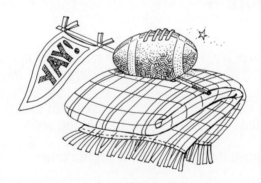

"Adopt" an older neighbor as a grandparent. Include them in the children's ball games and family outings...bake cookies together and share stories over dinner. Your family can help out by weeding flower beds, raking leaves and running errands. It's sure to be rewarding for everybody!

LUNCHBOX TREATS &
Party Desserts

Zucchini Brownies

Emilie Britton
New Bremen, OH

Before a family back-to-school party, I made these brownies as a trial run, but didn't tell my hubby about the zucchini. He ate the whole pan of brownies within 3 days! He gave me a funny look when I confessed...I just told him it was a new recipe, knowing he wouldn't have tried them if he knew they had zucchini in them. All is well now as he continues to enjoy these.

1/2 c. oil	1-1/2 t. baking soda
1-1/2 c. sugar	1 t. salt
1 T. vanilla extract	3 c. zucchini, finely shredded
2 c. all-purpose flour	1 T. butter, softened
1/2 c. baking cocoa	

In a large bowl, combine oil, sugar and vanilla; beat well with an electric mixer on medium speed. Add flour, cocoa, baking soda and salt; beat until combined. Batter will be very dry. Fold in zucchini by hand. Let stand for 5 minutes; batter should look wetter. If not, let stand 5 more minutes and stir again. Line a 13"x9" baking pan with parchment paper, creating "handles" at the sides; coat paper with butter. Spread batter in pan. Bake at 350 degrees for 25 to 35 minutes, until a toothpick inserted in the center is removed with crumbs but has no wet batter on it. Cool; cut into squares. Makes one dozen.

For perfectly cut brownies, refrigerate them in the pan
for about an hour after baking. Cut them with a plastic knife
for a clean cut every time!

Back-to-School
FALL RECIPES

Frost-on-the-Pumpkin Squares

Lynda Hart
Bluffdale, UT

This is my favorite fall dessert. The recipe was given to me by one of my co-workers many years ago and I've been making it every fall since then.

1/2 gal. vanilla ice cream,
   softened
15-oz. can pumpkin
1 c. sugar
1 t. salt
1 t. ground ginger

1 t. cinnamon
1/2 t. nutmeg
1 c. chopped pecans, toasted
36 vanilla wafers or gingersnaps
Garnish: whipped cream

Scoop ice cream into a chilled bowl; set aside to soften. In a separate bowl, combine pumpkin, sugar and spices; stir in pecans. Add pumpkin mixture to ice cream; blend well. Spread half of ice cream mixture in an ungreased 13"x9" baking pan. Arrange cookies over ice cream in a single layer. Spread remaining pumpkin mixture over cookie layer. Cover and freeze for at least 5 hours. At serving time, cut into squares; top with whipped cream. Makes one dozen.

Peanut Butter Popcorn

Margaret Hostetler
LaGrange, IN

This is a special treat that our three sons and their friends have enjoyed for years. Our sons are grown, but when they come home they have asked for peanut butter popcorn. I like to take this treat to parties whenever a snack is in order. Yum!

4 to 6 qts. popped popcorn
1 c. sugar
1 c. light corn syrup

1 c. creamy or crunchy
   peanut butter
Optional: 1 t. vanilla extract

Place popped corn in a large roasting pan; set aside. In a saucepan over medium heat, bring sugar and corn syrup to a rolling boil. Remove from heat; stir in peanut butter and vanilla, if using. Pour over popped corn and stir to coat. Cool; store in an airtight container. Serves 10 to 12.

LUNCHBOX TREATS &
Party Desserts

Forget 'Em Cookies

Glenda Anderson
Louisburg, NC

My mom made these cookies for my sister and me when we were little. When you bite into a cookie, it melts in your mouth! When I got old enough to bake by myself, I started making these cookies for Thanksgiving and Christmas.

2 egg whites
2/3 c. sugar
1/8 t. salt
1 t. vanilla extract

1 c. mini semi-sweet
    chocolate chips
1 c. chopped pecans

Preheat oven to 350 degrees. In a deep bowl, beat egg whites with an electric mixer on high speed until stiff peaks form. Gradually add sugar and salt; beat well. Add vanilla and mix thoroughly. Fold in chocolate chips and pecans with a spoon. Drop mixture by teaspoonfuls onto parchment paper-lined baking sheets, 2 inches apart. Place pans in preheated oven; turn off the heat. Leave in oven at least 3 hours or overnight before removing. Makes 3 dozen.

"Dirt" cupcakes are such fun for kids! Bake up chocolate cupcakes using your favorite recipe. When cool, top them with chocolate frosting and sprinkle with crushed chocolate sandwich cookie "dirt." Decorate with colorful gummy worms...eek!

INDEX

Appetizers & Snacks

Autumn Apple Dip, 164
Bar-B-Que Meatballs, 166
Best Mexican Dip Ever, 180
BLT Roll-Ups, 160
Brown Sugar Bacon Bites, 180
Cheddar-Sausage Cornbread Balls, 181
Cheesy Corn Dog Bites, 158
Chicken Pinwheels, 160
Corn & Bacon Chip Dip, 172
Crazy Crackers, 45
Crescent Roll Pizza Bites, 170
Devilish Ham & Cheese Log, 156
Fresh Tomato Salsa, 182
Garden Hummus Dip, 167
Guilt-Free Vegetable Dip, 157
Honey-Glazed Chicken Wings, 168
Hot Tots, 176
Karen's Crunchy Snack Mix, 162
Mild Buffalo Chicken Dip, 173
Parmesan Pretzels, 178
Pepperoni Pinch Me's, 161
Picante Salsa Dip, 158
Pizza Snacking Crackers, 178
Pumpkiny Fluff, 165
Roasted Pumpkin Seeds, 2 Ways, 163
Sausage Queso Dip, 159
Speedy Chicken-Salsa Quesadillas, 171
Spicy Snack Crackers, 179
Sports-Night Pepperoni Dip, 177
Sweet & Salty Pecans, 174
Thanksgiving Snack Mix, 174
Yummy Buckeye Dip, 164

Beverages

Berries & Cream Smoothies, 13
Blast of Sunshine Smoothies, 13
Caramel Apple Cider, 171
Harvest Punch, 175
Witches' Brew, 169

Breads

Ann's Sweet Cornbread, 44
Apple Corn Muffins, 57
Cheese-Topped Biscuits, 36
Dark Chocolate Chip Pumpkin Muffins, 8
Easy Pan Biscuits, 41
Mom's Banana Tea Bread, 21
Parmesan Bread Sticks, 51
Pimento Corn Muffins, 49
Pumpkin Spice Muffins, 53

Breakfasts

Amish Fried Apples, 24
Apple & Banana Griddle Cakes, 10
Apple-Filled Coffee Cake, 27
Beckie's Brunch Bake, 20
Beth's Egg & Chile Bake, 7
Chocolate-Banana Overnight Oats, 30
Cinnamon Pull-Aparts, 26
Cinnamon-Oat Granola, 12
Cranberry-Pecan Instant Oatmeal Mix, 19
Crescent Breakfast Squares, 14
Exciting Oatmeal Breakfast, 19
Fruity Breakfast Sundae, 12
Golden Waffles, 24
Ham & Cheese Breakfast Bites, 9
Ham & Egg Pizza, 6
Madge's Favorite Breakfast Bake, 15
Mama P's Sour Cream Pancakes, 26
Marshmallow Puffs, 28
Meat Lovers' Quiche, 14
Mini Breakfast Quiches, 23
Mini Egg & Cheese Bites, 25
No-Bake Energy Bites, 29
Omelet in a Bag, 32
Oven-Baked Cinnamon French Toast, 16
Overnight French Toast with Berry
  Sauce, 17
Peanut Butter & Jelly Pancakes, 11
Pumpkin Pie Baked Oatmeal, 18
Quick & Easy Home Fries, 7
Quick Avocado-Egg Breakfast
  Sandwich, 22
Sausage Breakfast Muffins, 22
Scrambled Eggs with Mushrooms &
  Swiss, 25
Skillet Breakfast Casserole, 31
Speedy Breakfast Burrito, 32

Cookies & Candies

Apple Butter Cookies, 203
Chocolate Chip Cookie Bars, 186
Chocolate Marshmallow Fudge, 210
Chocolate Poodles, 211

INDEX

Chocolate-Peanut Butter Haystacks, 209
Dressed-Up Popcorn Balls, 191
Forget 'Em Cookies, 217
Frost-on-the-Pumpkin Squares, 216
Frosted Pumpkin Cookies, 188
Good Boys Cookies, 187
Grandma's Pecan Toffee Bars, 193
Peanut Butter & Jam Bars, 206
Peanut Butter Balls, 210
Peanut Butter Bars, 184
Peanut Butter Popcorn, 216
Quick & Easy Halloween Bark, 211
Snickerdoodles, 213
Sour Cream Cookies, 202
Special Oatmeal Cookies, 213
Sugar Cookies Extraordinaire, 212
Sweet & Salty Crunch Cookies, 190
Zucchini Brownies, 215

Desserts

Apple Slab Pie, 198
Candy Corn Cupcakes, 195
Caramel Apple Cupcakes, 193
Caramel Apples, 201
Confetti Butterscotch Bars, 200
Cranberry Crunch Delight, 207
Cranberry-Pear-Apple Crisp, 197
Daddy's Pumpkin Custard, 204
Fresh Pear Cake, 196
Fruit Empanadas, 207
Glazed Cinnamon Apples, 214
Granny's Fruit Cocktail Cake, 189
Hayride Bundt Cake, 199
Homemade Doughnuts, 208
Indoor S'mores, 201
Mom's Chocolate Snack Cake, 185
Mother's Baked Apples, 205
Popcorn Cake, 194
Uncle Main's Pumpkin Pie, 192

Mains

After-School Pizza, 153
At-the-Ranch Chicken Tenders, 97
Bacon Cheeseburger Pizza, 124
Beans & Wieners Waikiki, 138
Best Grilled Chicken, 105
Black Beans & Rice, 148
Brian's Taco Pie, 146
Brianna's Pizza Pasta, 122

Butter-Roasted Turkey Drumsticks, 104
Caribbean Chicken, 90
Cheeseburger Crescent Pie, 150
Chicken in a Pot, 104
Chicken Lasagna, 116
Chile Relleno Casserole, 96
Chili Chicken Tacos, 154
Corn Chip Chicken, 96
Corn Dog Casserole, 136
Creamy Tortellini & Sausage Skillet
  Supper, 98
Crispy Fish Nuggets, 108
Easiest-Ever Chicken Tacos, 126
Easy Stuffed Shells, 111
English Muffin Pizzas, 134
Favorite Baked Penne, 94
Fiesta Skillet Dinner, 150
Florida Fish Tacos, 148
Fridge Fest Quesadillas, 149
Garden-To-Table Spinach-Alfredo
  Pizza, 123
Grandma Gigi's Pizza Sauce, 133
Hamburger & Potato Casserole, 107
Herbed Turkey Breast, 100
Homemade Coney Sauce, 139
Homemade Pizza Crust, 133
Italian Chicken & Rice, 89
Lemon Pasta With Broccoli, 109
Mediterranean Chicken, Spinach &
  Feta Pizza, 140
Mom's Beef Stroganoff, 92
Mom's Mexican Rice, 102
Nana's Taco Casserole, 125
No-Fuss Lasagna, 111
Not Your Momma's Fish Patties, 114
Our Family Favorite Casserole, 106
Pepper Jack Chicken, 120
Pierogies & Meatballs Casserole, 89
Pizza Spaghetti, 141
Poor Man's Beef Stew, 93
Pork & Rice Casserole, 113
Pork & Sauerkraut with Apples, 99
Quick Chicken Quesadillas, 151
Ranch-Style Casserole, 117
Roasted Italian Sausages, Peppers &
  Potatoes, 113
Sausage-Stuffed Pizza Peppers, 135
Shredded Pork Tacos, 127
Skillet Dogs & Potatoes, 131
Slow-Cooker Pizza Pizza, 152

INDEX

Southwestern Beef Tacos, 126
Spaghetti Hot Dish, 88
Spinach & Ziti Pasta Bake, 110
Steve's Macaroni & Cheese, 95
Super-Easy Chicken & Stuffing Bake, 91
Teresa's Oven-Fried Chicken Tenders, 97
Texas Spaghetti, 103
Upside-Down Pizza, 132
Yellow Squash Tacos, 127

Salads

Ambrosia Salad, 69
Bowtie Picnic Pasta Salad, 60
Broccoli-Raisin Salad, 61
Cauliflower Salad, 61
Easy Potato Salad, 66
Family Pasta Salad, 66
Fresh Cucumber Salad, 65
Holiday Apple Salad, 71
Lisa's Linguine Salad, 67
Pepperoni Pizza Pasta Salad, 64
Poppy Seed Garden Pasta Salad, 67
Salad on a Stick, 62
Saucy Golden Fruit Salad, 68
Sweet Carrot Salad, 63
Trish's Cranberry Salad, 70
Waldorf Salad, 69

Sandwiches

Bar-B-Q Beef Sandwiches, 119
Barbecued Hot Dogs, 128
Beef & Bean Pizza Burgers, 144
Chicken Ranch Sandwiches, 115
Chicken Veggie Burgers, 142
Chili Cheese Dogs, 129
Double Bacon Cheeseburgers, 143
Foil Dogs, 136
Hot Dogs Delicious, 145
Marcie's Rosemary Turkey Burgers, 142
Open-Face Franks, 130
Pizza Burgers, 144
Shredded Ham Sandwiches, 112
Southwest Turkey Burgers, 128
Steakhouse Burgers with Mushroom
    Sauce, 147
Sweet & Spicy Pork Sandwiches, 118
Teriyaki Burgers, 139
Western Burgers, 137

Sides

Butter & Honey Glazed Carrots, 81
Cabbage & Noodles, 85
Carly's Green Bean Casserole, 81
Carol's Crockery Beans, 78
Cheesy Broccoli-Cauliflower, 74
Cheesy Spinach Bake, 76
Corn & Zucchini Toss, 75
Country Filling Bake, 101
Creamy Corn, 75
Creamy Mashed Potatoes, 83
Creamy Vegetable Medley, 82
Granny's Sweet Potato Casserole, 80
No-Fry French Fries, 83
Oven-Roasted Potatoes, 77
Party Potatoes, 73
Pioneer Scalloped Corn Casserole, 79
Pumpkin Pie Applesauce, 86
Quick & Easy Rice Pilaf, 85
Spiced Apple-Stuffed Acorn Squash, 72
Sweet Potato Fries, 72
Tomato-Squash Sauté, 84

Soups

Beef Barley Soup, 37
Busy-Day, Lazy-Day Bean Soup, 44
Chicken & Vegetable Tortellini Soup, 35
Chicken Taco Soup, 42
Constance's Cabbage Soup, 53
Country Chicken Stew, 40
Country Soup Supper, 50
Cream of Bacon & Tomato Soup, 45
Easiest Beef Stew, 52
Good-For-You Chili, 34
Hearty Turkey-Vegetable Soup, 47
Italian Chicken Vegetable Soup, 54
Italian Sausage & Spinach Soup, 36
Meatball & Tortellini Soup, 55
Mexicano Chili, 56
Minestrone Soup, 38
Sassy Black Bean Soup, 39
Stone Soup, 58
Turkey Noodle Soup, 46
Tuscan Soup, 43
Vegetable Beef Soup, 49
Vegetable Soup for a Crowd, 48

Find Gooseberry Patch
wherever you are!

www.gooseberrypatch.com

Call us toll-free at 1·800·854·6673

U.S. to Metric Recipe Equivalents

Volume Measurements

1/4 teaspoon	1 mL
1/2 teaspoon	2 mL
1 teaspoon	5 mL
1 tablespoon = 3 teaspoons	15 mL
2 tablespoons = 1 fluid ounce	30 mL
1/4 cup	60 mL
1/3 cup	75 mL
1/2 cup = 4 fluid ounces	125 mL
1 cup = 8 fluid ounces	250 mL
2 cups = 1 pint =16 fluid ounces	500 mL
4 cups = 1 quart	1 L

Weights

1 ounce	30 g
4 ounces	120 g
8 ounces	225 g
16 ounces = 1 pound	450 g

Oven Temperatures

300° F	150° C
325° F	160° C
350° F	180° C
375° F	190° C
400° F	200° C
450° F	230° C

Baking Pan Sizes

Square		Loaf	
8x8x2 inches	2 L = 20x20x5 cm	9x5x3 inches	2 L = 23x13x7 cm
9x9x2 inches	2.5 L = 23x23x5 cm	Round	
Rectangular		8x1-1/2 inches	1.2 L = 20x4 cm
13x9x2 inches	3.5 L = 33x23x5 cm	9x1-1/2 inches	1.5 L = 23x4 cm